THE THOUGHT
AND ART
of ALBERT CAMUS

"Un petit traité, deux récits, un drame, une tragédie, quelques lettres, peu de pages, peu de mots, mais dans ce peu, l'homme moderne et son tourment, son péché, sa grandeur."

Rachel Bespaloff in
"Le Monde du condamné
à mort," Études, 1950.

THE THOUGHT
AND ART
of ALBERT CAMUS

THOMAS HANNA

HENRY REGNERY COMPANY

CHICAGO • 1958

Manufactured in the United States of America

CONTENTS

PREFACE

ALBERT CAMUS has now come into his own as one of the most prophetic, persuasive, and hopeful moral philosophers of the mid-20th century. It is not simply that he has assumed a central and highly influential role in the thought and letters of present day France, for this has been an accomplished fact for some time already; rather, it is now the case that the works of Albert Camus are eagerly awaited everywhere and are translated almost as soon as they first come into print. His significance is no longer just that of a Frenchman or even a European; it goes far beyond that. He is a world figure.

But, curious enough, it is also true to say that Camus is one of the most controversial and least understood of contemporary thinkers. The utter honesty with which he has accepted "his times," shared its destruction and nihilism, its fevered dream of happiness and universal peace—this honesty seems at first to be strange and incomprehensible. He has taken the mask off of recent history and shown us a world which we can recognize only with difficulty, perhaps because what he shows us is so intimately our own world. In France Camus has already inspired four different books explicating and interpreting his thought and art, and this is in addition to a small mountain of critical articles which have appeared continuously since about 1945. In England and the United States there have also been critical articles on Camus, and recently, full length studies have begun to appear. In the same proportion there is not, perhaps even among his admirers, a very far-reaching understanding in the English world of the full import of Camus' thought and art. In France and in Western Europe as a whole there is a wider appreciation of the scope of Camus' work, but even here certain confusions and misconceptions are continually evidenced which only emphasize the need for a thorough philosophical analysis of the *total* works of Camus, both literary and philosophical. The failing of the full-length studies on Camus in France is that they have either tended to see Camus too much as an artist or else they have soared off into the lyrical endeavor of making Albert Camus into a kind of living legend.

As one of the greatest of living French novelists, it is Camus' curious misfortune that the success of his novels has obscured the fact that he is primarily a philosopher who has projected this concern into all of his works. Until the scope of his thought is understood it will not be possible to appreciate fully the power and importance of his total works. Hence, there is a need in the French as well as the English world for a study which gives one a thorough acquaintance with all of the works of Camus in terms of the philosophical concerns which motivate them. Only by understanding Camus first as a philosopher can we fully appraise his literary works, for these literary works are part of a more general philosophical position and must be related to it.

It is the purpose of this book to present an analytical study of the thought of Albert Camus as seen in both his literary and philosophical productions. The constant themes, concerns, and principles which characterize these works will be indicated, so that we may determine whether the thought of Albert Camus has a philosophical coherence which can be documented, analyzed, and, finally, criticized. Such a study can be of value to those interested in Camus' literary pieces as well as to those concerned with contemporary philosophy. This is admittedly a sympathetic study of Camus' thought, but one that is characterized by a thorough internal criticism which indicates what is relevant to the structure of this thought, what is not relevant, and what are its contradictions. A more general comparative criticism is beyond our immediate concern; indeed, such criticism will be possible only after we have made the first step of understanding Camus' philosophy. This study of Camus' thought is presented with the conviction that Camus must be given a hearing, for what he says is of pressing importance for these difficult days through which the Western world must yet pass.

Except for a few key passages, all of the quotations made in this study from Camus and from French critical sources are rendered in English. In the discussion of *L'Etranger, La Peste,* and *La Chute* the English editions of these novels have been used, and in a few instances citations have been made from the English edition of *L'Homme révolté.* All other English translations made from Camus and from French critics are my own responsibility.

INTRODUCTION

IN THE COURSE OF A POLEMICAL LETTER, published in *Les Temps Modernes*, Jean-Paul Sartre heatedly said, "But I ask you, Camus, *who* are you to act so aloof?"[1] This is, of course, an appropriate question to raise. Sartre was faced with a man who would call himself neither Christian, nor Communist, nor existentialist, nor perhaps even French. Here was a man who held aloof from parties, creeds, and movements but who yet claimed to speak for the "human condition" and for "the oppressed." Who was he to speak for the oppressed? Where does he stand, and who or what does he represent? This man, Albert Camus, who was virtually unknown in France before the last war, has suddenly become the spokesman and judge of his epoch. With the mystery of a prophet, Camus has appeared and begun to speak, and his words have cut across institutions and ideologies with such an unexpected and incisive stroke that a startled audience has turned to him with much the same query as that of Sartre, "Who are you, Camus, to speak for our times and yet keep such a distance from the answers we have given to our problems?" Albert Camus stands alone and prophetic as "one of the most impenetrable among French contemporary writers."[2]

The sudden appearance of Albert Camus among the great voices of contemporary Europe was the occasion for the following remark by Pierre Néraud de Boisdeffre, i. e.,

At the time of the Liberation few people even knew the name of Camus; several weeks later two hundred thousand readers were admiring his anonymous editorials; today his influence can be compared with that of Sartre or of Malraux or else to that of Gide just after the First World War. . . . These works at first seemed to follow a path behind Sartre like a small barge trailing in the wake of an ocean liner; today we can wonder whether the disciple will take the place of the master, inasmuch as he has known so well how to express the drama of our epoch with an authentic art.[3]

This estimate of the place which Camus holds in French letters was written in 1950; since that time the influence which Camus has held in France has been consolidated by his most extensive philosophical work up to the present, namely, L'Homme révolté. Camus is now no longer a disciple, and it would be more correct to say that he never was such a disciple. The esteem in which he is held in France is due not to the fact that he has taken a place with the leading exponents of the French school of existentialism; it is due primarily to his attempt to surpass the contradictions in post-war existential thought and found a positive moral philosophy. Pierre-Henri Simon, in his series of lectures on the several 20th century conceptions of man, reserves the final lecture for Camus; his reasons for so doing emphasize the unique position which Camus' philosophy occupies. Simon chooses Camus for the final lecture

certainly not because he is the only person of his generation who is concerned with the human condition: Malraux has more pathetic meditations on the same subject, and Sartre a more extensive discussion. But, like Saint-Exupéry who would have had the same right to be heard last, Camus has not only sought for, but he has found the evidences of a way of salvation, he has set up the land-marks for a positive humanism.[4]

Albert Camus was born in Mondovi, Algeria, on the 7th of November, 1913. His mother was of Spanish blood; his father was a Frenchman and an agricultural worker who was killed in 1914 during the First World War. His graduate work was done in the University of Alger under difficult financial conditions, during which time he worked as an auto accessory salesman, as a meteorologist, as an employee in a ship-brokers concern, and for the *Prefecture*. He was, during this time, greatly interested in sports. His degree of *études supérieures* was awarded for a thesis relating Hellenism and Christianity. His doctoral studies were cut short by tuberculosis; during this illness there is evidence to believe that Camus was near death.

During these student days in Alger Camus established a theater group called *l'Equipe* in which he both acted and directed. Many of the plays presented by this group were banned, one of which, *Révolte des Asturies*, had been written by Camus on the instance of the miners revolt in Olviedo. He adapted several literary works for the stage, including *The Brothers Karamazov* and Aeschylus' *Prometheus*.

Somewhat later, Camus traveled extensively, in vagabond fashion, throughout Spain, Italy, and Czechoslovakia. All of these places are found as settings for some of his earliest works. His essays, *L'Envers et l'Endroit* (1937), and *Noces* (1938) are meditative pieces invoking the images of these countries. He became a journalist in Alger and, in 1939, in Paris where he remained until the war and occupation. He then joined the *Résistance* movement which took him first to Lyons and then back to Paris. In Paris he continued his journalistic work, publishing anonymous pieces and later becoming editor-in-chief of the newspaper, *Combat*, a position which he held until 1945; after this time he continued to contribute editorial pieces to the paper. His novel, *The Stranger*, had appeared in 1942, although it had been written some years earlier in Alger, when he was twenty-five years old. *The Myth of Sisyphus*, a group of philosophical essays, was published in 1943, and in each of the following two years he received wide acclaim for his plays, *The Misunderstanding* and *Caligula*. In 1947 Camus published *The Plague* which established him as one of the great French writers of the post-war period, and the many articles, editorials, and letters which he produced were followed in 1951 by *L'Homme révolté*, an essay which marked him as one of the great moral philosophers of the modern French period.

From the first moment that Albert Camus came into prominence in France, he has been classified as an existentialist philosopher, an allegation which continues to be accepted even today, especially by those who have come to know him only by his novels. This classification is something to which we should give some thought, inasmuch as Camus has never ceased to deny that he is either an existentialist *or* a philosopher. Whether Camus chooses to call himself a thinker or an essayist and not a philosopher is a matter of small importance. But the question as to whether or not he is an existentialist is something which should concern us as we begin this study of his thought. The simplest way of answering this question is to point out certain characteristics of existential thought and indicate whether or not they are shared by Camus.

Professor Jean Wahl, who is probably one of the most attentive students of existential thought, has attempted to point out some of the themes which are basic to this philosophy in his *Esquisse pour une histoire de "l'Existentialisme."*[5] According to Jean Wahl, there are two fundamental tenets of existential thought. The first of these is born in the realization that we exist without knowing the reason why; the formula for this is that existence is without essence. The second of these tenets is that because existence lacks essence it is constantly in danger and uncertainty, and especially does existence tend to call its own self into question in a ceaseless questioning which is directed outward to the world as well as inward to itself. It will become obvious in the course of this study that the authentic thought of Albert Camus does not embody these tenets for the reason that he does not find human existence to be without essence, which is to say that Camus' thought rests solidly on a certain conception of human nature. If one organizes his thought around the proposition that there is a human nature, and hence a given possibility of meaning and value in human existence, then these tenets of existential thought are incompatible with it. If there be a nature common to all men, this does not rule out the possibility that one's being may yet be uncertain and in question, but it does mean that the character of this uncertainty, its basis, and the reason for man's questing are clearly of a different order. Such is the case with the philosophy of Albert Camus: his thought seems to move in the same channels as that of Heidegger, Jaspers, or Sartre, but at its terminus it reveals its positive features and its substantially different character.

Once we are aware of this distinguishing feature of Camus' thought, then we may follow its development without confusing it with a fundamentally different body of philosophy. And it is quite true that Camus' works constantly deal with many of the secondary traits of existential thought, e.g., he opposes himself to the rationalism of classic philosophy which seeks universal and enduring truths or a hierarchy of values which is crowned by God; he believes that truth is found by a subjective intensity of passion; he maintains that the individual is always becoming and is constantly involved in choice, risk, and, thus, freedom; he recognizes the thesis that man exists *in* the world and is naturally related with it; lastly he is deeply concerned with the significance of death, its inevitability and its finality.

From Paul Tillich we may add two other secondary themes of existential philosophy, i.e., the conviction that philosophizing must begin with immediate personal experience, and, secondly, that there is a source of being which is more fundamental than the distinctions between objectivity and subjectivity.[6] Of these two themes, Camus shares the first but not the latter. We have said that Albert Camus is a moral philosopher, and he is almost exclusively this. He shows no concern for the ontological and epistemological experiments of Husserl, Heidegger, or Sartre. Nor does his thought tend toward an eternal "otherness" as does that of Kierkegaard and Jaspers.

He shares with all of these thinkers a common world of disunity and absurdity and a common human condition of finitude, suffering, and death, but the resemblance ends at this point. As early as 1945 Sartre had made the remark that Camus was not an existentialist, and, during the same period Camus had said that he and Sartre find their names associated so frequently that he would not be surprised if one day they were to insert a notice in the classified column to the effect that the undersigned will not be held responsible for debts incurred by the other.

Camus is associated with existential philosophy for another significant reason, which is his double role of philosopher and *littérateur*. Kierkegaard, Nietzsche, Heidegger, Sartre, Marcel, and Merleau-Ponty have all been inclined as much toward literary or dramatic expression as they have toward formal philosophical essays. Whatever their differences, all of these thinkers emphasize the emotional, dramatic, and existential aspects of human existence at the expense of the rational and abstract. And this brings us to the proper distinction to be made between Camus and the existentialists, as well as the proper comparison. All of these thinkers are concerned with the existential, but not all of them are existentialist philosophers. Sartre, for example, is an existentialist, because he has attempted to develop his existential reflections into a coherent ontology. Camus, Nietzsche, and Kierkegaard, on the other hand, maintain their thought in the existential without attempting to fix and define the nature of this flux.

At some time or other it has probably occurred to many persons that "existentialism" is a term which defies definition. If one says that Heidegger is an existentialist, then it is difficult to find anyone else who is an existentialist in these terms. At best it can be said that there are certain attitudes, concerns, and methods which can be generally characterized as "existentialist." But even this is not quite satisfactory. A philosopher may be a little more or less "existentialist," but this does not tell us a great deal. If we attempt, for example, to define the term, "romanticism," we can at best agree that this was an attitude dominant in the 19th century which often championed certain ideas and more often opposed other ideas, but we could hardly reach a satisfactory definition of terms. Even so, there is no disputing that Schumann, Delacroix, and Victor Hugo are "romantics." The phenomenon of existentialism is much the same; it is an attitude of the late 19th and 20th centuries which often champions certain ideas and more often opposes other ideas. Even as much of the 19th century is characterized as romantic, much of the 20th century may be characterized as existentialist. It is possible that Camus' own term, *la pensée révoltée*, may be more comprehensive than "existentialism."

In the last analysis, it is reasonable to conclude that the startling differences which set one "existentialist" off from another are explicable on the following basis: existential thinkers do not constitute a school, because their attention is not focused on certain rational concepts which are to be systematically developed; their attention is focused on the vagaries of their own immediate personal experiences as it reflects a world which has been profoundly transformed by the scientific criticism of the past three centuries. The existential attitude combines a thorough concern for the individual with an almost unbearable honesty in the description of that individual, his universe, and the history which molds him. It is because the focus of this attitude is on transitory experience rather than fixed principles, that its representatives all differ to the man. The similarity which they manifest comes from the fact that they share a common world and a common history. It is true that this attitude of mind has representatives throughout the history of philosophy, but at no time has there been such a general and concerted movement in the same direction. There is good reason for believing that out of the movement of existential thought there will come a dominant method of philosophizing which will find permanence long after "existentialism" itself has passed away. This would be a method of philosophy that requires that one incarnate what he thinks and that the truth of an idea be proved through the passion in which it holds and is held by the philosopher. This would be a philosophy which is valid only to the extent in which it takes the risk of binding itself to man in history.

Within this larger movement of existential thought Albert Camus is found. He, like many others, is a child of his times, and he openly accepts this relative position. His abiding concern is with the relation between man and his world, between men and their history. His thought is not to be systematized; at best it is to be described and then characterized. The unusual quality which he brings to us is his radical fidelity to the experience of contemporary men at grips with a universe and history which baffle and oppress them. He is that rare and precious individual in whom we see all of the contradictions and longings of an epoch held together in great tension. If he, holding on to these contradictions, can find hope, then we have made a step toward the "renaissance" to which Camus is dedicated. Friedrich Nietzsche felt himself to be the most acute conscience of nihilism of his times. Camus has learned much from Nietzsche, and it is by drawing a parallel between these two kindred spirits that we can best answer the question, "Who is Albert Camus?" It may well be that Albert Camus is the most acute conscience of the contradictions of our times between the nihilism of destruction and the nostalgia for peace.

PART ONE:

MAN, THE WORLD,

AND THE ABSURD

CHAPTER I
THE MARRIAGE FEAST WITH THE WORLD: THE YOUNG IDEAS

One lives with a few familiar ideas. Two or three. By the chance of worlds and men who are encountered, one polishes them and transforms them. It takes ten years to have an idea fully one's own—about which one can talk. Naturally, this is a little discouraging. But in this way man gains a certain familiarity with the beautiful face of the world. Up to that point he looked at it face to face. But then he has to step to the side to gaze at its profile. A young man looks at the world face to face. He hasn't had the time to polish the idea of death and nothingness, the horror of which, however, he has tasted.[1]

THESE words, written by Albert Camus during his twenty-third or twenty-fourth year, are prophetic of the type of modest development which within fifteen years put him in the position of being one of the most provocative thinkers to emerge from the post-war European scene. And true enough, these "few familiar ideas" are already sketched out in his *Noces*, a group of four descriptive essays depicting the Mediterranean world whose images never cease to haunt both the literary and philosophical works of Camus. But *Noces* not only presents us the themes that are native to Camus' thought; in *Noces* we discover the type of passionate thought that has come to be the characteristic of existential thinkers. It is difficult to read these four short essays without being reminded of the same rhapsodic prose that is the force of *Thus Spake Zarathustra*, a prose whose images continually espouse other

3

meanings, so that the symbolic and metaphorical quality of each image weights the essays with a sense of cosmic drama.

In *Noces* the youthful Camus writes of the images and sentiments which are invoked within him by the ancient North African villages of Tipasa and Djémila, of Alger and of cities of Northern Italy. In Tipasa, it is the picture of the Roman ruins near the village which are now covered and reabsorbed into the lush vegetation of the North African coastal regions. It is here that the foot-hills of Mount Chenoua move down to meet the sea. And it is here that the works of man's hands crumble and return to the earth. "In this marriage of ruins and spring the ruins have become stones once more and, losing the polish which man had given them, have entered again into nature."[2]

At Djémila it is the searing hot wind which batters against man until, weary, he abandons himself and becomes a part of its roaring, inhuman cry. Here the writer is fascinated by nature, not so much by its beauty as by its over-powering and indomitable force. The roaring wind which is the voice of nature is not friendly or familiar, it is not humanized, but rather it is strange, inhuman, and conquering.

At Alger it is not the city but its people and their life which interests Camus. The people of Alger are completely oriented toward life, this world, this body without this concern being hampered by intellectual or moral complications. All of their possessions are of this earth and hence they hold death in horror, because they are defenseless against it. It is the fact of death that is pointed up by the earthly naïveté of Alger. The most tragic of things is a happy man—this, because of death.

Through the art-galleries and cloisters of Pisa and Florence Camus continues his meditations on death and duration, purity and sin, hope and hopelessness. In Francesco's "Flagellation" we see the impassibility and grandeur of man frozen in the present, suffering, yet without hope. This, says Camus, is

4

what theologians call hell. In a burial cloister at Florence Camus strolls along reading, one after another, the epitaphs on the tombs. This person had possessed certain "virtues," that person had always fulfilled his "duties," another was a good husband and an acute business man. "Almost all, according to the inscriptions, were doubtlessly resigned to death inasmuch as they had accepted their other duties."[3] And an anger and revolt well up within him as he protests against such a resignation and satisfaction. For in face of the fact of death all of these virtues, duties and achievements were useless and came to nothing. Whatever an individual may do in life is useless because he must die. "But today still, I do not see that uselessness detracts from my revolt, and I well feel that it adds to it."[4] And thus a Florentine cloister poses the eternal problem of man's desire for duration and his destiny of death.

There are two convictions about which the prose of *Noces* winds all of its themes. The first is that nature or the world is distinct from and foreign to the understanding and desires of man, but is at the same time his home where he is fascinated, surpassed, and finally conquered. This conviction is developed in the Tipasa and Djémila sections. The second conviction is that death is the final and inescapable destiny of all men, and that man must adjust his life and actions to this inescapable destiny. This second conviction is the core of the last two sections entitled "Summer in Alger" and "The Desert." Within five years' time these two ideas were to have their implications logically and obstinately developed in *The Myth of Sisyphus*, published during the occupation in 1942. And within ten years the first of these convictions was to become less and less prominent, while the significance of death was to be probed deeper until the personal dimension gave way to the social dimension, wherein the significance of death becomes the guiding principle for a social and political philosophy. Camus may begin with only a few ideas which are really his own, but the ideas of man's divorce from the universe and the finality of death are such that when they are "polished" and "developed" their implications can be formed into a philosophy of life, albeit, as Camus would insist, a "modest" philosophy of life.

The fundamental convictions motivating the essays in *Noces* give rise to four other themes which are characteristic of Camus, and it is interesting to examine them in their earlier and more poetic setting. These themes are (1) the hopelessness of life, (2) the need to refuse the world without renouncing it, (3) purity of heart, and (4) happiness.

In "Summer in Alger" the earthly naïveté of the Algerians and their defenselessness before death gives rise to a reflection on hope, i.e.,

From Pandora's box, where swarmed the evils of humanity, the Greeks let out hope after all the rest as the most terrible of all. I do not know of a more moving symbol. For hope, contrary to what is believed, is equivalent to resignation. And to live is not to be resigned.[5]

In specific reference to the Algerians he says,

There are words that I have never quite understood, like that of sin. I think I know however that these men have not sinned against life. For if there is a sin against life perhaps it is not so much in giving up hope in it as it is to hope for another life and to rob oneself of the implacable grandeur of this life.[6]

If human life is a fraud when it is justified by hope, then the question arises whether one can live without appeal to God or hope, i.e., is suicide the logical response to the hopelessness of life? It is this question which constitutes the point of departure of *Le Mythe de Sisyphe*.

The theme of refusal of the world (a term later replaced by the word "revolt") rather than renouncement is Camus' vindication of the heroism and dignity of man. There is no better expression of this attitude in *Noces* than the following passage:

Few people understand that there is a refusal which has nothing in common with renouncement. What is the meaning here of the words future, improvement, position? What is the meaning of progress of the soul? If I obstinately refuse all of the "later"s of the world, it is because it is also a question of not renouncing my present richness. I do not like to believe that death opens into another life. For me it is a closed door. I do not say that it is a step which must be taken, but that it is a horrible and filthy adventure. Everything that is proposed to me endeavors to take away from man the weight of his own life. And before the heavy flight of the great birds in the skies of Djémila, it is exactly this certain weight of life that I demand and receive. To be whole in this passive passion, and the rest no longer belongs to me. I have too much youthfulness within me to be able to speak of death. But it seems to me that if I should it is here [in Djémila] that I would find the exact word which, between the horror and the silence, would speak of the conscious certainty of a death without hope.[7]

Here we have the early roots of the concept of revolt which later becomes the central moral principle of Camus' thought, after having supplanted the experimental principle of the "absurd" first developed in *The Myth of Sisyphus*.

The concern with human purity and innocence figures prominently in all of Camus' writings, especially in the literary works. Innocence is the expression of that sincerity with which we recognize ourselves as what we are. Innocence and honesty to one's self and condition are the basis for the integrity of the characters of Camus' plays and novels. Caligula's tyranny, Martha's unrepentant bitterness and Meursault's eventual revolt are fundamentally innocent. Purity of heart comes to all of them through their acceptance of themselves for what they are and their consequent demand upon the world and mankind to accept and welcome them for what they are and need. On a Sunday morning in the streets of Florence the young Camus describes the full-bosomed moist-lipped Florentine women and the flower stands in the corner of every church, loaded with dazzling flowers, in full bloom and glistening with flecks of water. And he makes the bemused observation that in these flowers as in these women there was a generous opulence, and I could not see that to desire one differed greatly from coveting the other. The same pure heart was sufficient in both cases. It is not often that a man feels purity of heart. But at least at that moment his duty is to recognize as true that which has so singularly purified him, even if this truth may seem a blasphemy to others . . .[8]

This is but a limited exploration into a larger conception of purity of heart, but it marks for us the direction of Camus' thinking. Camus seeks at this early period to defend the innocence of man, for sin is one of the "words that I have never quite understood." Man may attain to an innocence which cuts broadside across the code of the church or the state; this, because guidance and justification for human creatures comes neither from the heavens nor from the ruling of the state, but from man himself.

The universe which Camus has described is limited by death and man's estrangement from the world, and Camus calls for a refusal of the world which is not a renouncement and which means having the "conscious certainty of a death without hope." It is seen that a man may live such a life and retain purity of heart, but Camus goes on to add that such a life can also reach happiness. As we shall see, Sisyphus is a happy man despite his hopeless fate and Meursault is happy though death is about to cut short the absurdity of his own life. Even in these early meditations Camus has hold of a conception of happiness which is neither sensual nor transcendent but which seems essentially religious; a happiness which is the affirmation of the dignity and unique value of human life in a world which does not call man its own.

But what is happiness if not the simple accord between a being and the existence which he leads? And what more legitimate accord can unite man to life than the double consciousness of his desire for duration and his destiny of death? In this way one at least learns to count on nothing and to consider the present as the only truth given us by "grace."[9]

The two fundamental convictions of *Noces* and the themes which buttress them are, at this stage, merely meditative thrusts into what is later to become a moral philosophy. The rhapsodic prose of these early pieces, studded here and there with striking apothegms and touched with a certain anarchy, is a production of youthful brilliance. If it be true that prophets are ill-received in their homeland, it seems equally true that most prophets view their homelands with distaste and discomfort. It is more remarkable that Albert Camus, at the beginning of his literary production, expresses, not reaction, but love and understanding for the shores of North Africa, an understanding which becomes the setting for all of his subsequent thought. The attempt of a modern man to adjust his conviction of what is true with the natural and sensual beauty of the Mediterranean world: this is what Camus has attempted, poetically for the most part, in *Noces*. This adjustment must take place in the human heart, and, in the eyes of the twenty-four year-old North African, it involves *déchirement* and balance. And in this balance there is both human happiness and bitterness, the greater significance of which we shall see obstinately developed to its logical outcome in *The Myth of Sisyphus*. But for the moment

it is on this balance that we must stop: singular instant where spirituality repudiates morality, where happiness is born in the absence of hope, where the mind finds its reasons in the body. If it is true that every truth carries within it a bitterness, it is also true that every negation carries within itself a flowering of "yes." And this chant of love without hope which is born in contemplation can also become the most efficacious of guides for action.[10]

Thus, Camus spells out the task which is yet to be accomplished, and in a final phrase indicates the direction which he has chosen to pursue this task:

The earth! In this great temple deserted by the gods, all of my idols have feet of clay.[11]

9

CHAPTER II

AN ABSURD LINE OF REASONING

THE PROBLEM AND THE METHOD

THERE is only one truly serious philosophical problem: the problem of suicide. The meaning of life is the most urgent of all problems. The question is to know whether life is worth the trouble of being lived. "The rest, if the world has three dimensions, if the mind has nine or twelve categories, comes afterward. These are games: first of all one must answer."[1]

Suicide is not a social but a personal phenomenon. It is the avowal that life is not worth the trouble of being lived, that life is too much with us, that we do not understand it. And suicide is motivated by a sudden vision of the world without its ordinary illusions and trappings. Man suddenly finds himself a stranger to this world, like an actor exiled from his décor. This, says Camus, is the feeling of absurdity. The task, he says, is to examine the relation between suicide and the feeling of absurdity and to determine the degree in which suicide is the solution to the problem of absurdity.

Albert Camus addresses himself only to those who are concerned to put their actions in accord with their understanding of life's meaning. The passion, which was the dominant force in Noces, is now linked with the existential practicality of the philosophical task. These are serious and ultimate decisions which must be made in regard to the most fundamental of all questions of philosophy. But Camus counters this exigence by asking if one might find life to be meaningless and yet go on living as if it were not so. Also, there may be many persons who have committed suicide who do find life meaningful. Certainly the habit of the body to continue its life is just as important as any decision which the mind might take. So the question is again posed, i.e., can we find life absurd and go on living? Camus replies that this is possible, because a third element can be interposed between absurdity and death. This element is hope, which with death and absurdity makes the third theme of the inquiry. Hope can intervene and sustain life on the basis of future possibility. Hope is an *élision*, i.e., that which eludes the movement from absurdity to suicide.

With these three themes before him Camus proposes a method by which to analyze these themes. He proposes what he calls *"un raisonnement absurde."*

Does its [existence's] absurdity require that one escape it either by hope or by suicide? This is what must be clarified, pursued, and illustrated apart from all else. Does the absurd demand death? We must give this problem precedence over all others outside of any disinterested methods of thought and intellectual exercises. The nuances, the contradictions, the psychology which an "objective" mind can always introduce into any problem has no place in this research and this passion. The only thing required is thinking which is inexact, i.e., logical. This is not easy. It is always easy to be logical. It is almost impossible to be logical all the way to the end. Men who die by their own hands follow their feelings to the end of their thrust. Thus, reflection on suicide gives me the occasion to pose the one question which interests me: Is there a logic all the way to death? I can find out only by following in the unique light of evidence, without unruly passion, the reasoning whose beginning I am indicating here. It is what I call an absurd line of reasoning. Many are those who have started with it. I still do not know if they have held fast to it.[2]

This absurd line of reasoning is concerned with analysis, not knowledge. For any true knowledge is impossible. The most we can do is to note what we see and to feel the climate of a problem. There is a universe of emotions and sentiments within every human individual which can never really be grasped. But *practically* we can know a man by his acts and utterances, by his effect upon others as he moves through life. In a practical way the irrational feelings within men can be appreciated, analyzed, and defined. Hence, in the case of the Absurd, which can strike any man, it is a matter of enumerating all of the events and sentiments which accompany it. The feeling of absurdity itself cannot be grasped by anyone with clarity, but without plumbing the depths of man we can yet practically analyze such a feeling. The method which Camus proposes is that of the existential philosopher, entailing passion, interested involvement, and immediate *a posteriori* personal experience.[3]

THE ABSURD

The Absurd Walls: Spiritual and Intellectual Finitude

The birth of the feeling of absurdity is simple and sudden. It may happen to any man when the habitual chain of his daily movements is broken. A weariness with these movements may gradually appear, and then quickly the consciousness is awakened and the chain is broken. In this awakened state absurdity is seen as the discovery that one can no longer live for tomorrow and the future. The Absurd is a revolt against "tomorrow" and is the attempt to come to terms with the present. Once this awakening comes, the response is one of two things: suicide or readjustment. Camus has given us a description of these habitual movements which suddenly crumble, e.g.,

Rise, street-car, four hours at the office or factory, meal, street-car, four hours of work, meal, sleep, and Monday, Tuesday, Wednesday, Thursday, Friday and Saturday on the same rhythm, this route is followed easily most of the time. Only one day the "why" arises, and everything begins in this weariness touched with astonishment. "Begin," this is important. Weariness is at the terminus of the acts of a machine-like life, but at the same time it inaugurates the movement of consciousness. It awakens it and provokes what follows.[4]

What is the feeling that accompanies this "awakening"? With absurdity we find the world "thick and strange." Nature appears to be foreign and inhuman. Camus interprets this to mean that the structures, forms, and meanings with which we had hitherto clothed nature have now fallen away and nature is transformed and rebecomes itself before our eyes. The feeling of absurdity also reveals the foreign and inhuman aspects of other men, when their movements and actions are abruptly deprived of meaning. "In certain hours of lucidity the mechanical aspect of their movements, their meaningless pantomime, reveals the stupidity of all that surrounds them. A man speaks on the telephone behind a glass enclosure, one cannot hear him, but one sees his pointless mimicry: one wonders why he lives. This *malaise* before the inhumanity even of man . . . is also the Absurd."[5]

But if this awakening has revealed to us the foreignness of the world and even of other men, it does not find its full substance until the certainty of death is brought to mind. Certainly we know only the death of others, but for ourselves we possess that certainty of the "mathematical side of the event."[6] We know that death is the inescapable lot of all, and precisely because it is inescapable it renders all of life meaningless and futile.

Camus enumerates these things not as discoveries. These are not new experiences; they are well-known and oft-chronicled. But they must be spoken of to lay open the discussion of the *consequences* of these experiences. The question may again be posed: If the absurd revelation is true, then what can be done to escape it? Is the answer in suicide or in desperate hope?

Not only man's immediate personal experience is caught in the world's lack of unity and meaning, but also man's intelligence. A man is certain that he exists and that the world exists, but anything beyond this is construction. Even this certitude of one's existence cannot be justified or defined by the intelligence. Our minds desire to understand the world, to find unity in it, but the enumeration of events does not give us understanding. The mind discovers only paradox, and the nostalgia of man for unity ends against walls which cannot be hurdled, the "absurd walls" of the universe. This is our intellectual finitude. Camus sees three of these walls which thwart the needs of human intelligence, absurd walls which block the mind's search (1) for truth, (2) for unity, and (3) for a meaningful life based on hope.

The search for truth or falsity is the mind's primary task, but when the mind turns inward to examine itself it finds it is involved in contradiction. As Aristotle had already clearly demonstrated, if the mind affirms all as true, then it affirms at the same time the truth of the counter-truth that all things are not true. And if we maintain that all is false except that which we maintain is true, we still recognize an infinite number of true and false judgments, for not only are we maintaining a truth but we regress into another judgment when we maintain that what we are maintaining *is* a truth. The same type of vicious circle entraps the intellect when it seeks to affirm the unity of the world. This is because the affirmation of the world as one is possible only if the affirmer makes this judgment from a position outside of this unity, thus constituting an exception to this unity. The intellectual search for unity can only end in contradiction. The third failure of the intellect is its attempt to use hope as the foundation for a life of unity. There is always a cleavage between what a man thinks he knows and what he really knows about the world and about himself. Through hope a man attains unity in his life by acting on what he thus "thinks he knows." The failure of this attempt for living unity comes with the absurd revelation. At that moment the mind finds lucidity and comes to terms with that which it "really knows."

It is worthwhile to note that the first two of these "absurd walls" is given only cursory treatment by Camus. These purely logical exercises are foreign to Camus' thought as well as to the essential theses of his "absurd line of reasoning." It is man's immediate personal experience which is struck by the Absurd, and the mind's demand for logical consistency is comprised within this larger framework. What Camus wishes to establish is that this "sudden awakening" brings to light the confrontation of man's hopeless desire for clarity and unity, on the one hand, and the world's irrationality, disunity, and fragmentation on the other. The Absurd depends as much upon man as upon the world. The absurdity is in the confrontation of the two, for the world is not absurd, it is only irrational.

The uniqueness of Camus' *raisonnement absurde* is that he accepts the truth of the Absurd and maintains that if this be the truth then in all honesty we should be bound to follow this truth in all its consequences as well as to make it a guide of conduct. The "absurd line of reasoning" is an experiment in obstinate honesty and logic. It is this experimental character that makes for the interest as well as the tentative nature of Camus' essay on the Absurd. Commentators on this aspect of Camus' thought would do well to keep in mind his prefaced warning

. . . that the Absurd, accepted until now as a conclusion, is considered in this essay as a point of departure. In this sense one can say that there is a tentativeness in my commentary: the position which it takes should not be prejudged. One simply finds here a description, in pure state, of a sickness of spirit. No metaphysic, no belief is, for the moment, involved. These are the limits and the only definite position taken in this book.[7]

The importance of this warning cannot be exaggerated, inasmuch as Camus has been greatly misunderstood and "prejudged" because of his *Myth*. Those who misunderstand and attack Camus are legion, and this is an aspect of Camus' career to which we shall return more than once. But for the moment, let us re-emphasize the under-girding motive of both the early and later phases of the thought of Albert Camus: our century has been characterized by sickness of spirit, nihilism, and the feeling of absurdity, and we shall not come to terms with our times until we have analyzed and understood these phenomena for what they are. Several years after the writing of *The Myth*, Camus made the following similar remark which justifies his position and as well indicates some conclusions which we will not find in *The Myth* itself, i.e.,

> But what is true is that the *malaise* which concerns us is that of an entire epoch from which we do not want to separate ourselves. We want to think and live in our history. We believe that the truth of our century cannot be reached without going all the way to the end of our own drama. If the epoch has suffered from nihilism it is not in ignoring nihilism that we shall find the ethic that we need. No, all is not summed up in negation or absurdity. We know this. But first of all we must pose the problems of negation and absurdity, since this is what our generation has encountered and that with which we must come to terms.[8]

These words serve well to pre-warn and guide the reader on his first contact with the works of Albert Camus. He is not easily read nor quickly understood, and his preoccupations may seem queer and strange, but the moment we recognize that these preoccupations are not the products of Camus' imagination but are the given problems of our times, then we are willing to follow this experiment of *jusqu'au-boutisme*.

The Absurd as a Confrontation

Having recognized the truth of the Absurd, we must find out if, under these conditions, thought is possible. Camus replies that it is and always has been possible for thinking to go forward in absurdity, in this "desert." There have always been those who would defend the rights of the irrational, even as there has always been the struggle between rational and irrational thought. This perennial struggle points up humanity's schismatic desire for unity on the one hand and its clear recognition of the "absurd walls" on the other. But the attack against rationalism has never been so strong as it is in this day. And the body of irrational thinkers massed in this attack all have a common concern for a universe of contradiction, antinomies, anguish, and powerlessness, the type of universe which has been described by Camus as "absurd."

In the thought of Heidegger, Jaspers, Lev Shestov, Kierkegaard, and Husserl Camus finds irrational discoveries which strengthen and diversify this recognition of an absurd universe. All of these thinkers share a world lacking in unity, clarity, rationality, and hope. These men show that thinking is possible in the "desert," for therein lie some of human life's most pressing themes.[9] And thus Camus places himself in the tradition of these thinkers (though, as we shall presently discover, not with the conclusions of existential philosophy).

The central importance of the absurd experience having been emphasized, Camus turns from the feeling of the Absurd to the notion of the Absurd, from an exterior description to a direct analysis of whatever clear notion there is of the Absurd. This is in order that we may be more precise about the meaning of the Absurd, and hence set up our consideration of its consequences.

In simple terms the Absurd always involves a contradiction between a given state of affairs and reality itself, between one's intentions and the given possibilities, between an action and a world which is not in accord with that action. Obviously, then, the Absurd is not a fact which can be pinned down; it is a comparison between two things. The Absurd is neither one nor the other of its two terms; it arises from their confrontation, or, more precisely, from their divorce. Thus, the Absurd would increase as the contradiction increases between these two things. For the moment, then, we experience the Absurd as the unique and vital link between man and the world. And through the Absurd we know three things with certainty:

(1) what man desires, (2) what the world offers, (3) what unites man and the world. This is the triadic notion of the Absurd, and from this point of clarity we may ask what are the consequences.

THE CONSEQUENCES OF THE ABSURD

The immediate consequence of the Absurd is a rule of procedure, a ruling method inherent in the very nature of the problem. The Absurd is a problem having three terms. There is no absurdity without the world, and there is no absurdity without the spirit of man. Hence, the immediate consequence is that none of the terms can be dropped. This triadic notion of the Absurd is obviously an essential truth for me, and, as such, it must be preserved intact. The solution to the problem cannot be solved by destroying the problem itself. It is this problem which forces us to make a decision, to decide whether suicide is the logical consequence and solution of the Absurd. Once awakened to the absurdity of the world, we are faced with an unabating struggle in which there is a total absence of hope and in which there is our conscious dissatisfaction with and refusal of the world.

The Absurd is born of this confrontation between the human demand [*l'appel humain*] and the unreasonable silence of the world. It is this which must not be forgotten. It is to this that we must cling, because all of the consequences for a life may emerge from it. The irrational, the human nostalgia and the Absurd which is born in their *tête-a-tête*, these are the three characters of the drama which necessarily must be concluded with all the logic of which an existence is capable.[10]

The ruling method which Camus has indicated is essential in drawing out the consequences of the Absurd. Those who treat the problem of absurdity and negate one of its terms have not solved the problem but have merely escaped it. There are many who have done just this. These are the "existentialists" from whom Camus clearly disassociates his thought. These were the philosophers he had in mind when he remarked, concerning the *raisonnement absurde,* that "many are those who have started with it" but he was in doubt if any had "held fast to it." Thus, Camus marks a division between those who hold fast to the ruling method and those who do not. The latter group it is which commits "philosophical suicide" in drawing out the consequences of the Absurd.

Philosophical Suicide

All of the existential philosophers, mentioned earlier, recognize the problem of absurdity, but faced with the Absurd all of them seek evasion. Eventually they deify the very contradiction which crushes them and thereby believe to have found hope in it. In every case this forced hope is of a religious essence. This critical attack by Camus is of great interest not only for those interested in existential philosophy but also for the many who have seen in the conclusions of these thinkers the grounds for rejuvenating Christian theology.

Karl Jaspers recognizes the human impossibility of knowing the universe or of realizing transcendence and feels that we are "caught" in existence. Jaspers has no solution for the *impasse* with which he is faced, and without any justification makes a "leap" which affirms transcendency. For him the Absurd indicates that there *must* be somehow a transcendence of this absurdity. Hence, the Absurd becomes God. With Jaspers, the greater the contradiction, the greater his impatience and passion to affirm transcendence.

The Russian *émigré* philosopher, Lev Shestov,[11] in certain of his works, ends by recognizing the fundamental absurdity of human existence, but he does not say "This is the Absurd" but rather "This is God!" Camus has no quarrel with the mysticism of Shestov, but Shestov cannot claim to have remained faithful to the serious demands of the problem which he poses. For him, reason is vain, but there is something beyond reason. For the absurd mind, says Camus, reason is vain and there is nothing beyond it. Thus, Shestov drops one of the terms of the Absurd. The desire for rationality is negated and irrationality is absolutized. The problem of the Absurd is not solved but evaded. (Perhaps it will be worthwhile here to add that, in Camus' thought, the absurd mind recognizes the limited and useful rationality which is in nature, but this useful rationality explains nothing to him. Similarly, the absurd mind recognizes the irrationality which is both in himself and the world. The given terms of life are confronted. One must not have the uneasy suspicion that Camus denies that the sun rises and sets regularly and that the seasons revolve and the harvest can be expected. For the man "awakened" by the Absurd these things are obvious, but in turn he poses the Kierkegaardian query: "What does it mean to me?" A machine is perfectly orderly, but yet it is inhuman.)

Kierkegaard, also, finds the paradoxes and antinomies of life to be religious criteria. They are evidences of another world rather than the results of this one. He too flees the equilibrium demanded by the Absurd, negating the paradoxes in his desperate desire to find unity. Since nothing can be proved, then everything can be proved. And so, for Kierkegaard the fact of absurdity permits him to find hope in that which is contrary to hope: death. Even his God has the attributes of the Absurd: He is unjust and incomprehensible. More than this, Kierkegaard feels that the hopelessness (i.e., absurdity) of man's life is a state of sin. Camus emends this to say that it is a state of sin "without God."[12] If one asks Kierkegaard how we can live in this predicament, he replies that the predicament explains all, that our darkness is really light. He feels that if life is as absurd as this, then it is hopeless. But this means that he is refusing the given condition of absurdity. The

absurd mind will cling to this given condition, knowing that
to seek the truth is not to seek the desirable. Concerning
Kierkegaard's desperate affirmation of a transcendent unity,
Camus wryly concludes that "All things considered, a de-
termined soul will always work things out for itself."[13] But
Camus' more general protest against Kierkegaard is this:

I want to know if I can live with what I know and only with that.
Yet I am told that here the intellect must sacrifice its pride and
reason must give way. But if I recognize the limits of reason this
does not mean that I deny it, because I do recognize its relative
powers. I simply want to keep myself in this middle road where
the intellect can remain clear. If this be its pride, I see no reason
sufficient to renounce it.[14]

In Husserl and the phenomenologists Camus finds a philosophy which, in its first movement, affirms that thought is
a question of description, of seeing the world as it is. For
the phenomenologists there is no Truth but only truths, and
the consciousness fixes upon objects like a moving camera in
a succession without order where everything is equally important. This is a philosophy of an absurd universe where all
is to be experienced but not explained or transcended. However, Husserl moves away from the concrete by affirming that
the mind "intends" not only objects but "extra-temporal
essences." With Plato we have one essence for many objects,
but for Husserl there is an essence for each object. Even illusions are extra-temporal essences. In this way Husserl has suc-
ceeded in giving a fragmentary immanence and depth to the
universe, after having originally denied all transcendence. But
Husserl, in his turn also, goes forward to make the "leap"
which these other thinkers had made when he maintains that
these laws and essences attached to objects are eternal and
invariable, e.g., were there no minds, psychological processes
would still exist. At this point the Platonic essences have
moved into complete immanence, and while at first the inte-
grating power of human reason is denied, Husserl ends by

affirming an eternal Reason. The sense of the human condition (of the concrete) is thereby lost through an intellectualization which has generalized the concrete itself.

Whatever the method, rational or irrational, the religious philosopher pursues a path leading to the "leap" which solves all. For these men it is only a question of the will to arrive at this point. In Camus' estimation, the "existential attitude" tends toward the eternal. Its essentially religious character is that when its movement is negated it ultimately makes the "leap" into eternality. This is the pathetic pass to which these thinkers have come after their beginnings in a philosophy of meaninglessness.

If there is absurdity, it is in man's universe. The instant that this notion is transformed into a spring-board into eternity it is no longer related to human lucidity. The Absurd is no longer this evidence which man admits without consenting to it. The struggle is avoided. Man integrates the Absurd and in this union its essential character disappears, i.e., opposition, anguish, and divorce.[15]

These existential thinkers are more concerned to explain rather than to describe. Their nostalgia for unity is greater than their science. And although having used different methods, they all find the same reconciliation of their starting point, the Absurd. Camus concludes that reason can lead anywhere. Recognizing the problem of the Absurd, these philosophers have had to decide whether life can be lived under such conditions or whether the only answer is in suicide. There is fine irony in Camus' conclusion that the answer of the "existential philosophers" has been to deny thought itself and embrace that which negates thought, thereby committing "philosophical suicide" instead of suicide pure and simple.

For the absurd thinker, then, the existentialists have offered only that which contradicts the one truth that he clings to. The divorce which is his anguish and dissatisfaction cannot be transcended and then called inconsequential. It still remains. The Absurd has posed the question whether we can honestly live in this condition or must there be suicide. Philosophical suicide neither meets nor solves this problem.

Obstinate Absurdity: the Alternative Consequences

The Absurd is our one certainty. Everything may be refuted but not its three terms. There are two courses of action: we may escape this certainty through suicide, through the "leap," or through a tailor-made world of hope; or we may take upon ourselves the agonizing burden of the Absurd in which we unlearn to hope, cling to our lucidity, and remain in continual revolt against the world. Doing the latter is but a matter of persistence, of refusing the many religions of the world which offer escape through transcendence and which will accuse us of pride, of guilt, and of sin. But if anything, it is his innocence that the absurd thinker feels most strongly. His single desire is to know if one can "live without appeal" to something beyond human experience.

I do not know if this world has a meaning which is beyond me. But I do know that I am not aware of this meaning and for the moment it is impossible for me to see it. What could be the meaning for me of a meaning which is beyond my condition? I can understand only in human terms. That which I touch, that which resists me, this is what I understand. And these two certitudes, my appetite for absoluteness and unity, and the irreducibility of this world to a rational and reasonable principle—I know that I cannot reconcile them. What other truth can I affirm without falsehood, without interjecting a hope which I do not have and which means nothing within the limits of my condition?[16]

The alternative to suicide or philosophical suicide is an obstinate absurdity which is in constant revolt against the world. It is obvious that revolt is just the opposite of suicide. Suicide consents to the Absurd as final and limitless. Revolt is an ongoing struggle with the Absurd. Hence, revolt restores greatness to life; it is the beauty of the human mind at grips with a reality which exceeds it. Nothing is equal to this spectacle of human pride reaffirming itself in defiance of the world. Man must die unreconciled to the world, even as he has lived in defiance. *Revolt: this is the first consequence of the Absurd.*[17]

Secondly, for the absurd thinker the notion of freedom is seen in a unique light. For him there is no metaphysical problem of freedom. Freedom is ordinarily thought of as something given by God or some higher being, but in the light of the absurd revelation this no longer means anything to man. Freedom does mean something, however, when thought of in relation to the modern state and to the prison which constitute a living threat. Freedom is one of the essential gifts which the Absurd brings to light; an infinitely greater freedom than we had before.

The ordinary man lives on the basis of the future, working toward goals which are immediate as well as distant, and he believes that he is free in choosing these goals. But in the absurd revelation he realizes that he was conforming to given goals which seemed to be part of a non-existent larger meaning. To the measure that he had planned his life as if the world had meaning, to that extent had he lost his actual freedom. And thus it is that one of the first phases of this absurd freedom (and a point of departure for existential thought) is to call into question the commonly accepted goals and order of life. *The second consequence of the Absurd is this freedom*, the only reasonable freedom, because it is founded on the certainties of our condition, i.e., death and the Absurd. This is the only freedom that the human heart can live and feel.

The third consequence of the Absurd is passion. Once awakened, a man can live in this universe only with indifference toward the future and with the desire to exhaust that which is given in the present moment. If this world has no meaning for us, then there is no scale of values by which to judge our conduct. In an absurd universe Camus understands that "preference" does not exist. Our desire can no longer be qualitative but only quantitative. Our task cannot be to live better, but only to live more. Camus makes the interesting remark that our morality seems to be based on the quantity of experience which society makes available to its members.[18] He suggests that there may be an 8-hour-day morality even as the morality of the Greeks of antiquity was based on their leisure opportunities. However this may be, the central thought is that in an absurd universe a man is clearly aware of his coming death and, consequently, every present moment is precious. Quantitative experience is irreplaceable for a man whose destiny is death. "The present and the succession of presents before an ever conscious mind, this is the ideal of the absurd man."[19] In this third consequence of the Absurd, man at grips with a foreign universe has reaffirmed not merely his dignity but has moved farther in discovering a renewed passion in the heart of this absurdity. "Having begun with an agonizing consciousness of the inhuman, the meditation on the Absurd finds itself at the end of its itinerary at the very heart of the passionate flames of human revolt."[20]

Camus has offered us three rules for life, i.e., revolt, freedom, and passion; rules which are put forth, not in spite of the Absurd, but as the consequences of the Absurd for human life. Whereas this absurdity presented itself as an invitation to suicide, it has now, through obstinacy, been transformed into a way of life. Camus does not pretend that a life based on these "rules" is either inviting or completely rewarding; he simply maintains that only in this manner can men retain their honesty, lucidity, and dignity. These three consequences are the issue of the mind's meditation. The more important task is to make these things live.

THE ESTHETICS OF CREATION WITHOUT TOMORROW

The problem of interpreting and justifying the place of art

in the world is a matter of great concern for Albert Camus. As a writer he fulfills the roles of novelist, dramatist, and philosopher. The critical-analytical Camus has never ceased to re-evaluate the role of the literary Camus. In *Le Mythe de Sisyphe,* in the many editorials in *Combat,* in addresses and polemical letters, and in *L'Homme révolté,* in all of these instances Camus probes into the problem of esthetics. And it is in these instances that Camus' philosophical inquiry finds its most direct and practical expression. Camus, the philosopher, may permit himself a margin of impreciseness in other areas, but when it concerns Camus, the novelist, there can be neither vagueness nor indecision.

We have already indicated that the philosophy of Albert Camus must be considered in two separate sections. The analysis and tentative conclusions that emerge from this concern with the Absurd stand in a certain contrast to the later and more comprehensive philosophy of revolt. But whereas the general contrast between these two periods of thought is ill-defined, the specific contrast between the esthetics of these two periods is clear-cut. Because of Camus' dual role, his esthetic theory tells us more about his general philosophical position than any other area of his thought. It is because the philosophy of the Absurd found its full expression in an esthetics of the Absurd that Camus realized that a philosophy based on the Absurd alone was inadequate or, in any case, insufficient. The experiment was not a complete success, and adjustments were necessary.

This interplay between the philosophical and literary concerns of Camus is largely responsible for the richness and value of his writings. The primary crucible for his philosophical outlook seems to be the extent to which that outlook is compatible and fruitful for his life as a creating artist. At least so it seems to us. Having refused rationalism and the system, he has no other recourse than to begin with what he feels are certainties of his immediate personal experience and from there move forward by logical analysis and imaginative deduction. For a philosophy so conceived, the test is neither in its comprehensiveness nor in its consistency, for these are the criteria of rationalism. For such a philosophy the only measure of its adequacy is in living it, which is to say, by trial and error. If the philosophical enterprise is so conceived, then the philosopher must be prepared to adjust his thought, admit his errors, and continue resolutely to frame a philosophy which is justified in and by his life. Thought "weds itself to the experience of a life and there shapes itself."[21] The admirable feature of Camus' thought is its dead earnestness, its modesty, and its honesty in correcting itself when it seems to have erred. There is perhaps no philosopher of the mid-20th century with the sobriety, the honesty, and the persistence of Albert Camus. And consequently, there seems to be no philosopher on the current scene who stands in such isolation.

This is a necessary preface to a consideration of the esthetic theory of this, the early period of Camus' thought. Necessary, because, as will be seen later, Camus repudiates this theory in the chapter "Révolte et Art" in *L'Homme révolté* (1951). The general presuppositions of the *raisonnement absurde* are not negated but *transformed* in the later period, but the esthetic theory is cleanly contradicted.

The "absurd line of reasoning" has emphasized that to live with the Absurd is to cling to it with fidelity as the one certainty, the certainty of what man is and of what the world is. Only in the midst of this confrontation can man clearly see himself and the world. To be within the Absurd is a life-long wake of the lucid consciousness. The never-ending refusal of the world is the sole means of reaffirming the dignity of man. In *The Myth* Camus has supplied us with four examples of types of lives which can be lived in absurdity. These types are put forward not as recommendations; they are simply illustrations of the thesis that life can be lived in the consequences of the Absurd, i.e., in revolt, freedom, and passion. The first three of these types are Don Juanism, the actor, and the conqueror. These imaginative examples show how the absurd life may be lived and human dignity affirmed through innumerable loves, through mimicry, and through conquest. But the most important of these types is the last which is the "most absurd of the characters . . . the creator."[22]

If we are to maintain a lucid consciousness in face of the absurdity of the universe, works of art are of fundamental importance; they are the one means for man to support and sustain this consciousness. Through the mimicry of art we live not once but twice. There is no more *content* in art than there is in the acts of the lover, the actor, or the conqueror, but the important difference is that art has *fixity*. In this universe of inexhaustible quantity and diversity the essential for the artist as well as for the thinker is to describe. "For the absurd man, it is no longer a question of explaining or resolving, but of feeling and describing. All begins with a clear-visioned indifference. To describe: this is the ultimate ambition of absurd thinking."[23] As description, a work of art is simply another absurd phenomenon, but the difference is that here, for the first time, this personal awareness is brought out toward others and indicates their common lot.

In terms of the Absurd, Camus can see no distinction between the artist and the thinker, both of whom begin with absurdity and describe the world in their own individual manner. In both cases the most lucid of intellects is required, for the world must be described with *nothing added to it*. This is the goal of absurd art: that art mean nothing more than itself. Certainly, the artist may employ the richness of his own varied experience in the task of description, but he may not teach. Modesty is the goal. Description must understate. It must tend toward the less rather than the more.

This temptation to teach is of varying degrees according to the type of art involved. Music, more than all other arts, does not lend itself to teaching. It is in the novel that we have the greatest urge to teach and explain, and Camus poses the problem whether the Absurd can survive in the novel.

Like the philosopher, the novelist attempts to create a world. They both seek to fulfill this nostalgia for unity and clarity through the constructions of their own logic, ideas, postulates, and intuitions. In fact, the great novelists are philosophical novelists, i.e., they are not simply story-tellers but are creators of a universe. But can this creation take place "without appeal" to escapes which are beyond the ken of the Absurd? Can one avoid phantoms and create a world of palpable truths which cannot be denied? To do so is to remain faithful to the Absurd, eschewing hope, meaningfulness, and illusions. Camus contends that such a novel and such a universe can be depicted, and it would be such a work as would embody the same ambiguities and contradictions as certain of the philosophies of the Absurd. Exemplary of this type of novelist is Dostoievski.

All of Dostoievski's works posed metaphysical questions about the meaning of life and posed them with such intensity that the answer was *de force* that life was either false or eternal. Dostoievski is not simply a philosopher; his artistry is in illustrating what these questions and responses mean in human events. In *The Possessed*, Kirolov, in his own struggle with absurdity and ultimate death, is perfectly illustrative of the translation into life of the theme of absurdity. In Dostoievski's novels the Absurd is always the central question, be it in the problem of death or liberty or of exaltation. But, having posed the Absurd, Dostoievski finally betrays it. Both in *The Brothers Karamazov* and in the *Journal* he finds his solution in the "leap," this being the affirmation of immortality. In his novels men struggle against their hopes, but Dostoievski himself decides against his own heroes. He replies to the problem of absurdity, whereas the absurd novelist makes no reply. Is life false or is it eternal? Dostoievski replies that life is false *and* eternal. It is not Dostoievski's Christianity that contradicts the Absurd; it is his hope in future life. The central preoccupation of his novels is the absurdity of the Gospel, i.e., that men may be unbelieving in spite of and in revolt against their deep religious convictions. In sum, then, Dostoievski is not an absurd novelist; he is, according to Camus, an "existential" novelist.

From the example of Dostoievski Camus concludes that "creation without tomorrow" is painfully difficult. To create, as well as to live in the Absurd, requires of us an ascetic discipline *(une ascèse)*, for hope is difficult to elude even for those who so desire. Through the examination of these "existential" philosophers and novelists Camus feels that we have learned much about the Absurd, through seeing the aberrations which these men have made from a common starting-point.

Hence, this examination of absurd creation has brought to light a very particular type of art, an art without finality, i.e.,

Profound thought is in continual becoming; it weds itself to the experience of a life and there shapes itself. In the same way, the creative work of a man is strengthened by the successive and multiple visages that are put on by his separate works. One will complete the others, correct them, or recapture them, and also contradict them. If there is something that terminates creation it is not the victorious and illusory cry of the blinded artist, "I have said everything," but the death of the creator who closes his experience and the book of his genius.[24]

Camus sets himself against an art or philosophy which is satisfied. Absurd creation, like absurd thought must be shaped in revolt, freedom, and diversity. In these fleeting and "multiple visages" that proceed from the creator we see reflected the artist's disciplined and lucid consciousness which is their matrix. The artist, because he is living within the Absurd, recognizes that neither in his discipline nor in his works is there real meaning, content, or duration. In ten thousand years the works of Goethe will be archeological curiosities if they be anything at all. In the absurd flow of time a year and a millenium are equivalent; there is no seeking for eternity. And the artist is wisest when he can easily detach himself from his works. This in itself will make his work easier. All this is for nothing unless it be to aid the artist to banish his phantoms and live in clarity. But at least he is certain that this lucidity and this revolt are the one human dignity.

All thought which renounces unity, exalts diversity. And diversity is the field of art. The only thought that frees the spirit is that which leaves it alone, certain of its limits and its approaching end. No doctrine can entreat it. It awaits the ripening of works and of life. Separated from it, the former will once more make heard the scarcely muted voice of a soul forever delivered from hope. Or it will cause nothing to be heard if the creator, weary of his sport, intends to give it up. It is all the same.[25]

It was a question of obstinacy. And Albert Camus, with an intense and sober persistence, has shown us what it is like to live in a world forever caught in the web of the Absurd. For Camus, this is the truth which "carries within it a bitterness." We are bound in the midst of terrestrial faces, gestures, and dramas, and it is here that we shall find a difficult wisdom and a tomorrowless passion.

THE MYTH OF SISYPHUS

From the Homeric tales Camus has picked Sisyphus, the man who was condemned to the most terrible of punishments: eternally futile and hopeless labor. According to the traditions, Sisyphus was the wisest and most prudent of all mortals, who loved the earth and hated death and the gods. For some reason, an indiscretion with the gods or a trick played on Death, Sisyphus found himself condemned and in Hades. But through persuasion he was given one last stay on the earth. But once there, and having again tasted the "water and the sun, the warm stones and the sea," he no longer intended to return to the infernal shade and thus stayed with the sea and the earth. Enraged by such audacity the gods seized Sisyphus and dragged him off to Hades where his punishment awaited him. Sisyphus was condemned for eternity to roll a boulder up to the crest of a mountain from which it would, of its own weight, crash back down to the bottom.

What interests Camus is that moment when Sisyphus, having reached the summit, watches the boulder as it rolls back down the mountain-side and then trails downward himself to take up again his eternal torment. During this pause, which comes as regularly as his painful labor, Camus understands that Sisyphus has his hour of consciousness. It is in these instants that Sisyphus is superior to his destiny, stronger than his boulder. Sisyphus is conscious of his plight, and therein lies the tragedy. For if, during these moments, he nourished the hope that he would yet succeed, then this labor would lose its torment. But Sisyphus is clearly conscious of the extent of his own misery. It is this lucid recognition of his destiny that transforms his torment into his victory. The plight of Sisyphus is no more absurd than that of a modern laborer; and in the latter case there is tragedy only in those rare moments of similar consciousness. Powerless, and yet in revolt, Sisyphus is the proletarian of the gods.

Although these moments of descent may at times be painful, there may as well be moments when Sisyphus returns to his task with joy. It is in the full realization that he has seen his destiny for what it is that Sisyphus has become his own master. This night of the Absurd, which is as much a part of the universe as the yearning for light, the grains of this boulder, and the substance of this mountain, all of these things have formed the world of Sisyphus, beyond which he does not gaze. And in this subtle pivoting within him, by this revolt and scorn, Sisyphus has turned back to his world and, as master of his own life, stands facing a universe which no longer controls or deceives him.

AN ABSURD LINE OF REASONING

I leave Sisyphus at the bottom of the mountain! His burden is always there. But Sisyphus teaches the higher loyalty which denies the gods and moves boulders. It is his judgment also that all is well. This universe, henceforth without master, appears neither sterile nor futile to him. Every grain of this stone, every glistening mineral of this night-filled mountain forms a world for him alone. The struggle itself toward the summit is enough to fill the heart of a man. We must imagine Sisyphus as happy.[26]

CHAPTER III
THE LITERATURE OF
THE ABSURD

ALL of the novels and plays of Albert Camus are more or less direct dramatic expressions of his philosophical temper. It is wisest here if we emphasize the "less." Although we may find direct support for Camus' philosophy in his literary works, this, of course, does not mean that all of the ideas within his literary works find direct support in his philosophy. It is elementary to draw a line between the controlled, logical movement of a philosophical essay and the unpredictable, irrational, and hard to control movement of a human drama. Even so, Camus, like his talented countrymen, Jean-Paul Sartre and Gabriel Marcel, suffers misunderstanding at the hands of those who know only his literary productions and are content to infer from this the philosophical position. This fallacy of inferring the whole from the part has been the bane of contemporary French philosophy, but is the risk which any philosopher must run if he is to be a literary figure. Both Camus and Sartre (and Marcel in a lesser way) have found wide acclaim as novelists, and it is as such that they are known by their widest public. And it seems that the judgment of this public has been primarily founded on the ideas that they have gleaned from the reading of a few plays and novels. It is highly probable that the mountain of books, articles, and pamphlets that have been published attacking Sartre have been, for the most part, composed without a reading of Sartre's *L'Etre et le Néant*. But Sartre's excellence as novelist and playwright and the seven-hundred page bulk of his ontological essay make such an outcome inevitable. Moreover, existential philosophy is even betrayed by many of its own professed adherents who commit this same fallacy, such that the expression "existentialist" has come to mean for the French public something synonymous to the literary and pseudo-religious movement of Dadaism which followed the First World War.

Our concern, then, in examining the literary works of Albert Camus, is to find support and illustration for his philosophical position. We should not attempt to find in these literary works hidden ideas which would correct or shed unexpected light on this philosophy. If it be possible to discover a "thesis" within these works, then this should be an expression of his own philosophical concerns. That which remains is the human drama itself and the images and sounds of the world: the literary sphere which is not relevant to our immediate task. Much has been said about Albert Camus from the point of view of literary criticism and appreciation; it falls to us here to make explicit those principles and concerns that make up the fixed structure of Camus' thought, which is to say, his philosophy.

We have divided this study of the philosophy of Albert Camus into two periods: the early concern with the *Absurd*, and the later concern with *revolt*. His literary works correspond to the same division. There are three works which fall within this earlier period: the novel, *The Stranger* and the two plays, *The Misunderstanding* and *Caligula*. In these works we have a literature of the Absurd.

THE STRANGER: A NOVEL

Meursault's mother has died. She had been living at an old people's home not too far distant from Alger, and Meursault goes there to attend the funeral. During these last years he had seen his mother but little; they had followed separate lives and "had nothing else to say to each other," and Meursault, weary and somewhat bewildered, sits through the wake and then passively follows what is required of him during the burial rites. Directly after the funeral he returns to Alger. The following day he goes swimming, meets a girl he had once slightly known, goes with her to a comic film, and then takes her home with him for the night. The next day, Sunday, was passed in boredom; evening came and the week-end was over. Monday would come and all would take up again. Mother was buried, Sunday was over and, as usual, work began on Monday. "Really, nothing in my life had changed."

Meursault continues to see Marie, his girl friend. Also he indifferently accepts the proferred friendship of Raymond, a resident of the same apartment building and reputed to be a panderer. Meursault agrees to write a note to Raymond's former mistress, an Arab girl, so that Raymond could carry out a perverted plan of revenge for her infidelity. The plan is carried out, the girl is beaten and there are police involved. Raymond asks Meursault if he will vouch for him to the police that he had good cause for beating the girl. Meursault has "no objection" and agrees to this also. Through an acquaintance of Raymond, Meursault and Marie are invited to the beach. While there they discover that an Arab, the brother of Raymond's former mistress, is waiting near the beach hut, and apparently intends to avenge his sister. There is a fight. Later, Raymond, carrying a gun, goes back to the same spot. Meursault goes with him and is handed the gun while Raymond attempts to begin another fight. But they return without incident. Meursault does not wish to go back into the hut and returns to stroll along the beach in the searing midday heat and light. He is drawn back to the big rock where the Arab had been; there is a little spring which pours from the rock and flows toward the sea. But the Arab is still there. Meursault moves toward the coolness of the rock, numbed by the heat and glaring light; the Arab draws a knife, Meursault grips the revolver still in his pocket, the Arab's knife catches the reflection of the sun. "A shaft of light shot upward from the steel, and I felt as if a long, thin blade transfixed my forehead." Meursault fires the revolver; the Arab falls, then Meursault fires four more shots.

Meursault is arrested, arraigned for murder and the trial comes after a year in prison. During the trial the prosecutor descibes Meursault as a hardened, unfeeling criminal; he had sent his mother away to a public home, visited her rarely, had not shed a tear nor desired to see her body during the wake and funeral, had smoked and drunk coffee during the wake and had not lingered at his mother's grave following the burial. Moreover, the day following his mother's death Meursault had gone swimming, had seen a comic film and had begun an illicit romance. And Meursault's friendship with an underworld figure such as Raymond fully indicated his criminality. It was Meursault who centered in the whole affair: it was he who wrote the letter, it was he who testified for Raymond, it was he who carried the gun toward the very spot where he knew the Arab lay, it was he who fired five shots into the Arab's body. What was Meursault's defense? He "tried to explain that it was because of the sun,"[1] but he could not get across what he really wanted to say, and he heard the "people tittering" in the courtroom. Meursault was found guilty and sentenced to be decapitated "in the name of the French people."

This is the story of the "stranger," yet there is more, much more, involved. This is a résumé of the individual events that lead Meursault to his sentence of death. These innocent and careless acts have suddenly been gathered together, interpreted by a prosecuting attorney, confirmed by a jury, and Meursault is recognized as a "monster" whose death has been decreed by society. He has "learned that familiar paths traced in the dusk of summer evenings may lead as well to prisons as to innocent, untroubled sleep."[2] The rest of the story involves Meursault's adjustment to his destiny of death and his eventual revolt. But this we shall return to in a moment.

Our main concern with *The Stranger* is to determine whether Meursault is or is not a hero of the Absurd, in the sense in which we have come to understand in *The Myth of Sisyphus*. If he is, then we have in *The Stranger* a full and dramatic representation of the themes and consequences of the Absurd, a dramatic example of those "absurd types" (Don Juan, the actor, the conqueror) which were only sketched out in *The Myth*. Jean-Paul Sartre, for one, feels that this is the case. In his "Explication de *L'Etranger*," which is a critique of both *The Stranger* and *The Myth of Sisyphus*, he maintains that Camus' novel is an attempt to express the *feeling of the Absurd* whereas *The Myth* attempts to present the *notion of the Absurd*[3] Sartre gives open praise to this novel which "in the midst of the literary production of our times . . . was itself a stranger."[4] Sartre admires not only the originality but the technique and craftsmanship of the work, i.e.,

. . . bit by bit the work organizes itself under the eyes of the reader, it reveals the solid sub-structure which supports it. There is not one useless detail, not one which is not taken up by what follows and thrown into the discussion; and, the book closed, we understand that it could not have begun otherwise, that it could not have had another ending: in this world which is presented to us as absurd and whose causality has been carefully weeded out, the smallest incident has weight; there is not one which does not help to lead the hero toward the crime and toward the capital penalty. *The Stranger* is a classic work, a work of order, written about the absurd and against the absurd.[5]

This is high praise, and it is no doubt buttressed by Sartre's presumption that the novel is the direct literary expression of the philosophical principles of the Absurd. But although Sartre sees the philosophical and literary works of Camus as two sides of the same coin, still he is disturbed by the fact that Meursault does not revolt until the last pages of the book, and hence is not an absurd hero except for a brief moment in the novel.[6] This lack of coordination, that Sartre perceives, is explicable not by the fact that Camus has missed his mark but rather because Camus was not specifically aiming for this mark when he wrote *The Stranger*. Because of the proximity of publishing dates of *The Stranger* and *The Myth of Sisyphus* (both were published in 1942) Sartre felt that the latter work was an explanation and justification of the former. But this is somewhat of an injustice to Albert Camus. The actual completion of *The Stranger* was in 1939, a year before completion of *The Myth*, but close analysis of the novel will show us a substantially greater separation between these two works, inasmuch as *The Stranger* fully reflects a state of mind which was still exploring the ideas we see germinating in his early essays, *Noces*.[7]

Hence, if we are to understand this first of Camus' novels in relation to his philosophical position, we must not, as does Sartre, thrust it into a framework which was not fully spelled out at the time. There is no doubt that the themes of the Absurd are here present, i.e., absurdity, revolt, a refound freedom and the transforming significance of death, but with attentive study it becomes obvious that these themes are presented in a dramatic pattern which does not conform to that ideal pattern which is suggested in *The Myth*.

In considering Camus' "absurd line of reasoning" we have discovered that "tout commence par la conscience et rien ne vaut que par elle."[8] The problem and threat of the Absurd does not arise *until we have become conscious of it*, until the "awakening." This is what Sartre and still others have neglected in their studies of *The Stranger*. In terms of Camus' later position, Meursault is a paradox, because from the beginning he shows the absolute indifference of the absurd hero, but at the same time does not possess the absurd hero's consciousness of the absurdity of his life and the revolt against it. This latter stage does appear but only in the last moments. With this bit of clarity in mind we can see *The Stranger* within its own proper structure.

It is Meursault's indifference that, from the first moment

till the last, makes him a stranger to the world. Following his mother's death, nothing had really changed in his life. When Marie asks if he loves her Meursault says "that sort of question had no meaning, really." She asks him to marry her, and he replies again that "it had no importance really, but if it would give her pleasure, we could get married right away." His employer offers him an alluring position in Paris, but Meursault is indifferent to the proposal. He indifferently accepts Raymond's request to write the letter and later agrees to testify for him before the police. Even after the murder this attitude prevails. He is not interested in having a lawyer, nor does he show any concern before the trial. And, finally, after the condemnation, Meursault admits this indifference to himself as he thinks over the picture which the prosecutor had drawn of him, i.e.,

Of course, I had to own that he was right; I didn't feel much regret for what I'd done. Still, to my mind he overdid it, and I'd have liked to have a chance of explaining to him in a quite friendly, almost affectionate way, that I have never been able really to regret anything in all my life. I've always been far too much absorbed in the present moment or the immediate future, to think back.[9]

All of these instances, as well as this final avowal, take place before Meursault's "awakening." Meursault *acts* like he is in an absurd universe but is not *conscious* of being in an absurd universe or of the consequences which this entails.

From our privileged position of following the story through the eyes of Meursault himself, we move with him from one moment to the next, haunted by the feeling that something is strange but yet at every instant *understanding and sympathizing* with his choices and actions. Moreover, no one else is disturbed by Meursault's conduct; neither Marie, nor Emmanuel, nor Celeste, nor Raymond, nor Masson, nor Salamano. Within this drifting, monotonous rhythm of work, love, sun, and sea, they live together with an easy and sympathetic tolerance. Here, Meursault is no more a stranger than Marie or Salamano. On this level of the ordinary, humdrum life Meursault is really no different from any man. From this point it could have been *any man*, not just Meursault, who was to be judged and condemned by society. But what has happened is that this drifting life has carried Meursault to an action which was *to force a judgment* upon him. Because of his crime, a clear and absolute judgment must be made on the life of Meursault; an absolute moral criterion must be introduced into his life and an unequivocal judgment passed. The movement of the story is abruptly transformed by the introduction of this new element: the necessity to pass a moral judgment. From this point on, the world with which we were in sympathy (that of Meursault or Marie or *anyone*) is thrown into contrast with the world of the legalists, of the ethical absolutists.

Caught in this web of the absolute judgment, Meursault continues to be what he is: indifferent. Whereas, heretofore, Meursault has not been seen as strange, now he becomes so. Immediately after his arrest, Meursault's lawyer is dismayed and vexed by his client's nonchalance. Meursault's honest expression of his indifference convinces the examining magistrate that he is a "case hardened" criminal. During the trial, the prosecutor seems sincere in describing the accused as a heartless monster. And in listening to the prosecutor's remarks and in watching the faces of those in the courtroom, Meursault finally realizes that he is a "stranger" to this world of absolute moral standards, to-wit:

His tone and the look of triumph on his [the prosecutor's] face, as he glanced at me, were so marked that I felt as I hadn't felt for ages. I had a foolish desire to burst into tears. For the first time I'd realized how all these people loathed me. . . . On stepping into the box he [the doorkeeper at the old people's home] threw a glance at me, then looked away. Replying to questions, he said that I'd declined to see Mother's body, I'd smoked cigarettes and slept, and drunk *café au lait*. It was then I felt a sort of wave of indignation spreading through the courtroom, and for the first time I understood that I was guilty.[10]

The fragmentary and individually understandable events in Meursault's life were united under a moral judgment, and Meursault realizes that such a life under such a judgment means guilt. He did not feel that he was a criminal, although he could see that he came under that description; even so "it was an idea to which I never could get reconciled."[11]

In recapitulation of what we have thus far determined, we can say with certainty that the hero of *The Stranger* is not exemplary of or explained by the principles later sketched out by Albert Camus in *The Myth of Sisyphus*. The fact that Meursault lives with the indifference of an absurd hero but lacks the consciousness and revolt of the absurd hero, shows us that the philosophical clarity of *The Myth* is not yet here present. Those who have tried to make a direct correspondence between the novel and the subsequent philosophical essays succeed only in confusing the proper structure of this novel, which deals with the Absurd, but in a manner which is independent of the essays. In this review of the indifference which characterizes Meursault and of that moral absolutism which forcibly crushes him, we come to see that the absurdity which is pictured to us is not that of man before a senseless and fragmentary nature which is foreign to him as a human being; the absurdity is in the attempt of society to justly apply absolute moral standards to the uncertain and chartless course of human life. It is not an absurd universe which destroys Meursault; it is a moral legalism which has injected fixed values into a sphere which has no fixed moral values, i.e., human life. *The Myth of Sisyphus* has uncovered the divorce between man who desires unity and the world which is in fragmentation both for the intellect and for the immediate personal experience. *The Stranger* has shown the divorce between the attempt to live honestly in accord with the indeterminate character of human existence and the attempt to interpret that human existence in general moral terms of absolute validity. *The Stranger* is nearer to the concerns of *Noces* than to *The Myth of Sisyphus.*

The central act of this short novel is Meursault's murder of the Arab. It is this act which ushers in the whole mechanism of moral legalism and sets up the absurd contrast between what we know Meursault to be and what the court decides that he is. Understand that it is not the murder which is in question during the trial; there is no doubt that Meursault killed the Arab. The question during the trial is whether Meursault's life shows him to be a man who is a "case hardened" criminal. Camus has brought about the perfect absurd situation where Meursault (or anyone) is seen to have lived a life which *proves that he is guilty.* It is not the murder which proves his guilt; it is his life which proves his guilt. This is to say that any life, placed under the judgment of absolute moral standards is guilty and monstrous.

It remains for us to understand clearly that Meursault, in committing murder, still retains the innocence which has characterized him from the beginning, which is to say, the act of murder was consonant with all of the other actions which indifferently issued from Meursault.

Why did Meursault shoot this man whom he did not even know? The answer is, in fact, that it was "because of the sun," but there is no way to justify this in a legal proceeding when all acts are explained by willful intentionality. Of one thing we have no doubt: that Meursault's eyes are extremely sensitive to bright light. This is indicated to us no less than fourteen times previous to the murder.[12] Added to this is Meursault's own state of mind during the outing on the beach. During the lunch he had drunk too much wine and was "slightly muzzy."[13] This state of mind is amply suggested during the encounter which Meursault and Raymond had with the Arab a few minutes before the final encounter when Meursault faces the Arab alone:

The sun glinted on Raymond's revolver as he handed it to me. But nobody made a move yet; it was just as if everything had closed in on us so that we couldn't stir. We could only watch each other, never lowering our eyes; the whole world seemed to come to a standstill on this little strip of sand between the sunlight and the sea, the twofold silence of the reed and stream. *And just then it crossed my mind that one might fire, or not fire—and it would come to absolutely the same thing.*[14]

At this moment Meursault is more deeply aware than ever of the meaninglessness and indeterminacy of human life and of the complete lack of relatedness between himself and this other man. When Meursault returns to the hut with Raymond he has no desire to go inside, and so returns to stroll on the beach in the heat and glare of the midday Algerian sun. From this point on we are aware of nothing but the agonizing play of heat and light in the confused consciousness of Meursault, and of his inordinate compulsion to return to that one spot of coolness on the beach: the large rock from whence the spring trickles. The Arab was still there, "a blurred dark form wobbling in the heat haze."[15]

The heat was beginning to scorch my cheeks; beads of sweat were gathering in my eyebrows. It was just the same sort of heat as at my mother's funeral, and I had the same disagreeable sensations— especially in my forehead, where all the veins seemed to be bursting through the skin. I couldn't stand it any longer, and took another step forward. I knew it was a fool thing to do; I wouldn't get out of the sun by moving a yard or so. But I took that step, just one step, forward. And then the Arab drew his knife and held it up toward me, athwart the sunlight . . . I was conscious only of the cymbals of the sun clashing on my skull, and, less distinctly, of the keen blade of light flashing up from the knife, scaring my eyelashes, and gouging my eyeballs. Then everything began to reel before my eyes, a fiery gust came from the sea, while the sky cracked in two, from end to end, and a great sheet of flame poured down through the rift. Every nerve in my body was a steel spring, and my grip closed on the revolver. The trigger gave, and the smooth underbelly of the butt jogged my palm. And so, with that crisp, whipcrack sound, it all began.[16]

Meursault has at last brought to light the secret of his indifference and the reason for his unchanging attitude even in face of death. It is because death is the foundation of this indifference. This "dark wind" in the future of all lives gives us an absolute freedom; a freedom that does not license anarchy but which means that no matter what we do it has no final importance, whether crime or sanctity. Meursault has shown his *revolt* against the illusion of moral absolutism, he has reaffirmed his *passion* for the irreplaceable present moments of life and he has become conscious of the boundless *freedom* that death grants to the living.

The chaplain gone, Meursault is calm but exhausted. He sleeps. When he awakes "the stars were shining down on my face. Sounds of the countryside came faintly in, and the cool night air, veined with smells of earth and salt, fanned my cheeks. The marvelous peace of the sleep-bound summer night flooded through me like a tide."[18] Meursault has found peace. He thinks of his mother and understands why she, in her fading years, had taken a *"fiancé"* and tried to make a fresh start of life at the home for old people. "With death so near, mother must have felt like someone on the brink of freedom, ready to start life all over again."[19]

And I, too, felt ready to start life all over again. It was as if that great rush of anger had washed me clean, emptied me of hope, and, gazing up at the dark sky spangled with its signs and stars, for the first time, the first, I laid my heart open to the benign indifference of the universe. To feel it so like myself, indeed, so brotherly, made me realize that I'd been happy, and that I was happy still. For all to be accomplished, for me to feel less lonely, all that remained to hope was that on the day of my execution there should be a huge crowd of spectators and that they should greet me with howls of execration.[20]

Through the "dark wind" of death Meursault has found peace with the world and unity with his fellowmen.

We have dealt at length with this first novel of Albert

Camus, not only because of the wide esteem which it merits, but also that we may relate it clearly to his philosophical concerns. We have seen that it is not to be explained and structured according to the *Myth of Sisyphus*. Many of the same principles found in *The Myth* are in evidence in *The Stranger*, and we have noted that in the closing moments of the novel Meursault "awakens" to his revolt, liberty and passion. The ideas are simply put forward as a triumphant reply to what is inevitable, and they are yet to find their form and coloring in the later essays. But what is most obvious is that Meursault is not revolting against the absurdity of the world; rather, he is revolting against the attitude which holds that human life is to be governed and judged according to autonomous principles which are lasting and sovereign. Meursault cannot be found in *The Myth*; he is found in *Noces* walking through a Florentine burial cloister and in revolt against the pretention of those righteous and accomplished men and women who now lie in ashes and nothingness. Sustaining the same fervor that we found in *Noces*, Camus has rejected eternal values which themselves are strangers to this world and can but oppress us. Rather than revolting against the absurdity of the universe, quite the contrary, he revels in and gives himself up to "the benign indifference of the universe" and the "marvelous peace of the sleep-bound summer night." In *The Stranger* Camus clings to the beauty of this world which is strange, fascinating, and conquering and from which we are snatched by the "dark wind." *The Stranger* and *Noces* belong to that authentic thrust of Camus' philosophy which, after passing through the experiment of the *raisonnement absurde*, refinds its channel and fuller development in the philosophy of revolt.

THE MISUNDERSTANDING: A PLAY

Leon Thoorens, in his interesting study of the early phase of the thought and works of Albert Camus, has aptly observed that, as a playwright, Camus belongs to that category of writers who are "trop intelligent."[21] In his plays we see that Camus has sacrificed the container for the content and, consequently, has produced uneven dramas which often project a message that does not always seem integrated with the dramatic situation itself. The first two plays written by Camus are expressions of his own concern with the Absurd. Both of them possess some fine dramatic moments, but, on the whole, tend to leave an audience bewildered. This criticism is less apt for the two later plays, *L'Etat de Siége* and *Les Justes*, which are clear and forceful expressions of his philosophy of revolt.

The Misunderstanding,[22] which was first produced in 1944 had already been presaged in *The Stranger*.[23] Hence, we know that this story interested Camus as early as 1938. The incidents of the tale are widely known, and it is probable that some such happening did take place in Czechoslovakia. The story is that of a son who returns, after twenty years absence, to his mother and sister who own a small inn. The son is now rich and has come to share his wealth with his long-neglected family. He arrives at the inn and requests a room, but does not disclose his identity. Neither the mother nor daughter recognize him. Seeing that he is wealthy, the two women decide to murder the man, even as they had previously done to other solitary travelers. During the night he is murdered; the following morning they discover his identity, and both mother and daughter kill themselves.

The deadly irony of this tale was probably what first attracted Camus. Moreover, the tale itself poses the question as to the difference between murder of a stranger and murder of a son. In the play, the mother and Martha, the daughter, receive Jan as the single guest in their village inn. Jan, the son, has with him his wife, Maria, whom he persuades to stay in another inn for the night, although Maria does not like the idea. By remaining unknown for awhile Jan thinks he will be able to "see them a little from the exterior. I can see better what will make them happy."[24] At the right moment Jan will reveal himself and tell his mother and sister that he has come to take them with him to his own home which is on the sea. We have here a favorite contrast for Camus: the dark, cloudy interior of Europe and the sun-drenched beaches of the Mediteranean. Jan speaks of Europe as if it were another land, and there is little doubt that Jan's home is in North Africa.

Jan is the emissary of the Mediterranean, but the two women do not know that he has come to them. The misunderstanding begins to form when we learn that Martha lives only for the time when she can leave this heart of Europe and live out her days by the sea. It is this dream that is the motive for the several murders that have already taken place, and with the wealth of this new guest they will have enough money to fulfill the dream. Martha says,

Oh Mother! When we have built up a great sum of money, and we are able to leave this land without horizon, when we leave behind us this inn and this rainy town, and when we forget this shadowy country; the day when we shall finally be before the sea of which I have so dreamed, on that day you will see me smile. But it takes a lot of money to live easily by the sea. It is because of this that we must not fear words. It is because of this that we must make ready for him who is to come. For, if he is rich enough, my freedom will perhaps begin with him.[25]

From the beginning, the final tragedy is apparent. They do not know that this new guest has brought them the one thing they desire and will willingly offer it to them. Jan's reticence to present himself immediately as the son provides the misunderstanding which introduces horror into what otherwise would have been the salvation of the two women. Leon Thoorens justly remarks that this is reminiscent of the Christ who was killed by those to whom he brought the good news.[26]

The two women are careful to find out their guest's exact situation and whether he has friends in the town or is expected by anyone in the near future. Jan replies that he is alone and no one expects him. The son, seeking to learn more about his mother and sister, plies them with questions about their personal lives. The daughter, especially, rebuffs these questions, knowing that the less they know about the intended victim the easier will be the murder. Here again, for hidden reasons, each is in conflict with the purposes of the other. Jan is able to learn nothing about his family and is disappointed that all of his questions seem to annoy his sister. "In face of this taciturn young girl I vainly seek for the word which will reconcile everything. And since everything is less difficult for her, it is easier to find the words which reject than to formulate those which reunite."[27] But it is no less difficult for Martha to rebuff Jan's questions. Holding fast to her vision of the sea, she attempts to fend off the open friendliness of the guest. In spite of both their efforts, both women are attracted by the gentleness and innocence of this stranger, and both become less fixed on their plan. The mother seems to sense some common bond between this man and herself and prefers to wait a little while longer before going ahead. But Martha will not permit of indecision which might rob her of the one thing for which she lives. She assures her mother that "this will be tonight or not at all."[28]

Briefly, during the second act, Martha relaxes her defensiveness and listens, enrapt, while Jan tells her of the warm and open coast which is his home. For his own part, Jan is telling her of the land where he will take Martha and her mother, and he is inwardly pleased with her obvious fascination. But for Martha's part, these stories have the effect of galvanizing her in her desperate plan to leave this "shadowy land." Jan, hoping to create dreams which he would soon make real, has, unknowingly, created the resolution in Martha which will assure his death.

Shortly afterward, Martha brings the guest the tea which is drugged. While drinking the tea Jan decides that his plan has failed and that he will leave that evening, return to Maria, and then the following morning come back to the inn with his wife and announce that he is the son. Presently, the mother knocks and asks if he had drunk the tea. She had wanted to foil Martha's sudden decision to go ahead with the murder, but, seeing that the tea had been drunk she recognizes that it is too late to go back. Later, as the two women sit quietly by the sleeping Jan, the mother admits that she had wanted to prevent him from drinking the tea.

Yes, I came up here when you told me that tea had been brought to him. He had already drunk it. If I had been able to, I would have prevented it. But when I understood that everything had just begun, I gave in to the idea that we could go through with it and that, after all, it wasn't greatly important.[29]

The mother's remark is the same as Meursault's when he said that to fire or not fire at the Arab "would come to absolutely the same thing." We see that both of these women live in a world which is oppressively absurd, where death is seen as inescapable and where death by murder or death by fate comes to "absolutely the same thing." The mother accepts these ideas passively, even as Meursault had done. But Martha uses this attitude as a reason for action. With death waiting in her future, she realizes that only the present moment has value, and the wretchedness of her present condition warrants any action which can give her the irreplaceable experience of the sun and sea. This guest has fallen into their hands, and now he is to learn that "this room is made for one to sleep in and this world for one to die in." And then she adds "Come, Mother, and for the love of this God which you sometimes invoke let's finish with it."[30] The mother and daughter then carry the son to the river where he is drowned.

At the beginning of Act III the two women are disposing of all the personal belongings of the guest. His passport is discovered. Martha reads it, and then calls her mother who also reads it. The "misunderstanding" is now in the open, and the mother's response is to follow her son to the river. She knows that life is meaningless, but this new discovery is more than she, an aged woman, can cope with. Not to have recognized her son grieves her, but to know that the son still loved her and had returned for her gave rebirth to her love for the one whom now she would never again see.

> That proves that, in a world where everything can be denied, there are undeniable forces and that, on this earth where nothing is assured, we have our certitudes. (*With bitterness*) A mother's love for her son is now by certitude.[31]

And then she says,

> This is nothing other than the suffering of being reborn to love, and evenso it is too much for me. I know too that there is not even any reason for this suffering. (*With a new accent*) But this world itself is not reasonable, and I can well say this, I, who have tasted it from creation to destruction.[32]

The mother goes to her death for the love of her son, and the daughter is left alone.

If the mother has given in to the absurdity of the world and found death the better choice, this is not so with Martha. She is sustained by an angry revolt against her mother as well as her brother. Her dream of the sea is still there, and what does it matter if his death was necessary for this to be realized. After all, he had lived there; he, at least, had tasted these joys which she had never seen. And the death of a man is a vain reason for this one joy to be taken away from her, after it has already taken away her mother. This is the anger of the child who stayed home while the Prodigal reveled: a parallel which Camus wishes to indicate when he has Jan call himself the "Prodigal."[33]

With her mother gone, hatred now wells up within Martha, who is left alone and forsaken. Without her mother she realizes that she could never find her dream, not to mention the impossibility of explaining to the police what had happened. She is trapped and is

... too far from that which I love, and my distance is without remedy. I hate him, I hate him for having found what he wanted. For a country, I have this thick, bounded spot where the sky is without horizon, for my hunger the bitter plum of Moravia and nothing for my thirst except the blood which I have shed. This is the price which must be paid for the tenderness of a mother! ... Let her die then, since I am not loved!

And then Martha bursts out with a clear expression of revolt against an absurd and unjust universe, i.e.,

Let me hold on to my rightful anger! For before I die, I shall not raise my eyes to implore Heaven. ... Oh! I hate this world where we are reduced to God. But I, who suffer injustice, I have not been rightly dealt with, and I will not kneel. And deprived of my place on this earth, rejected by my mother, alone in the midst of my crimes, I shall leave this world without being reconciled.[39]

This could not be Meursault speaking, he who opened himself to the "benign indifference of the universe"; this anger of Martha is the anger of an absurd hero who accuses the world and will not be reconciled. Martha is directly expressive of all of the principles of *The Myth of Sisyphus* but one, to-wit, she commits suicide. But even this is explicable for the reason that suicide is the alternative to death at the hands of society. In Martha, the experiment of the *raisonnement absurde* has already begun, and we see that it has led to death.

The remainder of the play brings us the confrontation of Martha with Maria, Jan's wife, who comes to find her husband and is told quietly by Martha that he is dead and that they have killed him through a "misunderstanding." Maria is horrorstricken before such madness and injustice, but Martha rejects any accusation of crime. Maria has lost a husband and Martha has lost a mother as well as her one hope: *les comptes sont reglés*. And if Maria must look to her God for help then

"Pray your God that he make you like stone . . . this is the only true happiness."[35] For Martha, the choice is between suicide or the living silence and muteness of the stones. There is no place in this world for hope and desire; the world prevents it and in the end affirms its triumph in death. These words of Martha immediately recall similar passages in *Noces*, when Camus, speaking of the hills of Djémila writes that "In this great confusion of wind and sun which mixes light in with the ruins, something is forged which gives to man the measure of his identity with the solitude and silence of the dead city."[36] And later he writes: "The measure of Man? Silence and dead stones. All the rest belongs to history."[37]

Martha leaves, intent upon her own death, and Maria remains, alone and completely without help. She kneels and prays God for mercy. The old housekeeper of the inn, a man who has remained totally silent throughout the play, hears her cries and comes in to ask if she had called him. She turns to the old man, pleading for help in the same manner in which she had pleaded to God. The old man's reply is simple and firm: "No!" Maria remains alone in a strange universe, among strange and incomprehensible people, with her arms vainly raised to the empty heavens.

Le Malentendu is a drama which concerns the life of desperate and confused people who attempt to fulfill their hopes in an absurd universe and are defeated by a foolish misunderstanding. From the point of view of the philosophical thought of Albert Camus this play is intimately involved with the desperate and obstinate thought of *The Myth of Sisyphus*. Camus presents Martha and her mother not as ideal examples of how to live in an absurd universe; he offers them as dramatic examples of two persons clearly aware of such a universe, who suffer from it, struggle against it and are finally defeated by it. But here the question arises, even as it has in *The Stranger*, as to the innocence of these people. In both instances a detestable act has been committed, but Camus does not condemn them. Camus has dramatically pushed the confrontation of man and the Absurd to a terrible extreme, and has left us to decide whether these people are not still innocent. If not, then what are the grounds for their guilt?

CALIGULA: A PLAY

The four-act play, *Caligula*,[38] is a highly interesting work of much greater merit than its predecessor *Le Malentendu*.[39] It would be well if we would think of both of these plays as carrying the warning which had prefaced *Le Mythe de Sisyphe*, which is to say that what follows has a provisional character and hence should not be prejudged as having taken a final position. And the warning might be extended to say that the preoccupation with the Absurd is an experimental attempt to take the experience of the Absurd seriously at its face value and dispassionately draw out all of its consequences, whatever they may be, and perhaps therefrom we shall learn something. In *The Misunderstanding* the Absurd was seen to issue in murder and suicide on a limited scale; in *Caligula* the Absurd gives birth to murder, destruction, and madness on an almost universal scale. Even so, the latter is a comedy, and it is perhaps one of the most terrifying comedies ever written. *Caligula* is a gay, almost lighthearted, comedy of the Absurd. Like all comedy it finds its source in conflict and destruction of things which are not of ultimately serious importance. But its uniqueness, in this respect, is that, in taking the Absurd as its point of departure, nothing is seen to be of ultimately serious importance, which means that the conflict and destruction are universal and yet persuasively comic. Thus, we say that this is a terrifying comedy, and one which, for all of its dramatic excellence, is calculated to leave its audience uneasy and somewhat bewildered.

Drusilla, the sister of the emperor, Caligula, has died, and the young emperor has suddenly disappeared. Caligula, who has lived with Drusilla in incest, apparently is thunder-struck by this loss. He has been missing for days and the patricians are gathered in the palace somewhat worried about the outcome of this unexpected reaction of the young ruler. Caligula eventually returns, disheveled and tired, and he is anxiously questioned. He says that he is tired for having walked a great deal. Then he says that "It was difficult to find." And the questions and answers run as follows: "What was?"—"What I wanted."—"And what did you want?"—"The moon."—"What?"—"Yes, I wanted the moon."—"Ah! Why?"—"Well, it's one of the things which I do not have."—"Quite so. And now is everything arranged?"—"No, I wasn't able to have it."—"That's annoying."—"Yes, that is why I am tired."[40] If there is any doubt after this that something has changed in Caligula, this is immediately dispelled when Caligula says,

But I am not mad; in fact I have never been so reasonable. All of a sudden I simply felt a need for the impossible. (A pause) Things as they are don't seem satisfactory to me. . . . I didn't know it before. Now I know. (Always naturally) This world, as it is made, is not bearable. Hence, I need the moon, or happiness, or immortality, something which perhaps is crazy, but which is not of this world.[41]

The play has begun with death, and Caligula has tasted this death and discovered the absurdity of human existence. Death is "only the sign of a truth which makes the moon necessary to me. It is a truth which is quite simple and quite clear, a little stupid, but difficult to discover and heavy to carry." This truth is that "Men die, and they are not happy."[42] From this truth, discovered by Caligula, the comedy proceeds. This is the truth which is shared by the youth in the Florentine cloister, by Meursault, by Martha: it is the realization that the inescapability of death renders all things equally transient and unimportant to us, and that this equal value or equal

57

valuelessness means that we have a boundless freedom. Caligula is emperor, and thus his freedom is absolute.

> . . . everything around me is falsehood, and I desire that people live in the truth. And quite rightly I have the means to make them live in the truth. For I know what they lack, Helicon. They are deprived of knowledge, and they lack a professor who knows what he is talking about.[43]

In this pedagogy of the Absurd Caligula proceeds to destroy the order as it exists. If *tout est équivalent*, then men must no longer be deceived by the illusory value of the present order and customs. Caligula's decrees are intended to destroy all sense of preference and discretion, so that wrongness becomes so confused with rightness that neither is meaningful in society. In this way men will live in the truth, the truth of the absurdity of human existence, and Caligula will have fulfilled his task as "professor." From the point of view of his own motives Caligula is neither evil nor tyrannical; he is a "just" man, an "idealist" who follows his ideas relentlessly and courageously.

Caligula's new reign is one of capricious decrees of executions, famine, extortion, and immorality. He dresses himself as Venus and forces his subjects to donate a money offering for the privilege of seeing a goddess. He takes the wives of the patricians, and others he sends to the *maisons publiques*. He involves the patricians in ridiculous poetry contests of which he is the sole judge. In the middle of the night they are summoned to the palace to witness a brief and ludicrous dance by Caligula who has desired to communicate an "artistic emotion" to them. Those who do not appreciate the dance are to be decapitated. Caligula has brought his subjects completely under the sway of arbitrariness, confusion, and absurdity.

The "absurd line of reasoning" finds its fullest dramatic expression in *Caligula*, but we should not seek to discover any additional concepts to buttress what Camus has written concerning the Absurd. What is striking is that within the play there is voiced an opposition to this reign of absurdity which both understands the Absurd and yet rejects it as rule of action. This, in effect, is what one has expected from Camus and what he himself has sought for in his thinking about the Absurd: a response to the Absurd which recognizes its place in human experience, but yet finds a constructive basis for an honest and hopeful life in such a universe. Against Meursault there was arrayed the opposition of the legal moralists. Against Martha there is the indignant Maria who turns to the empty heavens. But against Caligula there is formed an opposition which draws its strength not from eternal values, nor from sanctified social institutions, but from a defense of needs which are felt native to human existence. Cherea, the confident as well as enemy of Caligula, puts forth this position when Caligula asks him why he refuses to give himself to the absurdity of human existence, i.e.,

Because I desire to live and be happy. I believe that one can be neither one nor the other by pushing the absurd into all of its consequences. I am like everyone. To feel myself free, I sometimes wish for the death of those that I love, I covet women which the laws of family or of friendship forbid me to covet. To be logical I would have to kill or possess. But it is my judgment that these vague ideas are not important. If every one tried to realize them we could neither live nor be happy. Once again, it is this that matters.[44]

Caligula's response to this is that Cherea believes in some higher idea; this would place Cherea in that large category of men who condemn the idea of absurdity in the name of God or eternal values. But the important thing is that Cherea will not be placed in this category. It is not a higher idea which makes Cherea oppose Caligula, but simply because he believes that "there are actions which are more beautiful than others."[45] All actions are not equivalent, and a judgment of them can be made without invoking the aid of sources beyond human experience.

At this point we have crossed the threshold, which takes us beyond man's experience of the Absurd and introduces us to the philosophy of revolt. In 1945, the same year in which this play was produced, Albert Camus published his *Remarque sur la révolte*.[46] This essay and the play, *Caligula*, are the summation of Camus' philosophical experiment. The experience and notion of the Absurd are no longer the center of concern; this has been surpassed by the experience and notion of revolt. It is interesting that this higher concern found such early literary expression (1938) and such late philosophical expression.

What we must bear in mind is that Cherea's revolt is in the name of something which *does not transcend* Caligula's philosophy of absurdity; *it surpasses the absurdity of life*. In this sudden shift we have not abandoned the standpoint of immediate personal experience but simply broadened it. The question, "Can we live without appeal to sources beyond our condition?" has not changed. The excesses of a life lived solely in absurdity have brought to light an essential dimension of human experience: revolt. From this point onward, Camus is to analyze, explore and expand this principle, first suggested here.

It is revolt which destroys Caligula. In pursuing his reign of absurdity, Caligula has run against something he did not know existed, to-wit, *limits*. He acted with the understanding that his freedom was limitless and thus inaugurated the kingdom of the "impossible," but he is destroyed by the rebellion of those who believe he has transgressed limits which man can not bear to have transgressed. What this means is that in a world without God we are not delivered into absurdity and destruction. This world has no hierarchy of values, rooted in absolute transcendence, but it does have bounds against which man cannot long transgress. Caligula, in the end, realizes that the ambitions of man are governed by limits in the universe and limits in the nature of men. In face of death he realizes that *he is not innocent,* nor is he justified, i.e.,

Caligula! You also, you also, you are guilty. Well, isn't this so, a little more a little less! You see now, Helicon did not come. I shall not have the moon. . . . Everything seems so complicated. Even so, everything is so simple. If I had the moon, if love sufficed, all would be changed. But where quench this thirst? . . . I know, however, and you know also (he extends his hands toward the mirror, sobbing) that it would be enough if the impossible existed. I sought it in the limits of the world, in the confines of myself. I reached out my hands (crying), I reach out my hands, and it is you that I meet, always you in face of me, and to you I am full of hatred. I did not go the way that was necessary, I ended with nothing. My kind of freedom is not good.[47]

With the movement of a Greek tragedy, *Caligula* has shown us a man who believes himself to be following a course of action which is true and courageous, only to discover at the end that what he has done is clearly wrong and is to turn upon him and destroy him.

Robert de Luppé, in his study of the works of Albert Camus, has made the following observation which emphasizes the experimental nature of *Caligula,* as well as *Le Malentendu.* He says,

The drama of the absurd, bolder than *Le Mythe de Sisyphe,* thus describes the ruinous consequences of the discovery made one day "on the corner of a street": it is a theatre of violence and of murder. . . . Camus, who has been given the stage of a theater as Caligula has an empire, makes experiments which he does not endorse. He allows the absurdist logic to move straight forward, observes its point of termination which is crime or madness, then seeks the fault, the imperfection. *Caligula* is a field study for the theorist of *L'Homme Révolté.*[48]

With *Caligula* this field study comes to a close; the experiment has borne its bitter fruit, and has pointed out the limitations and excesses of the absurd line of reasoning. The peculiar immediacy of the problem of the Absurd has made it necessary that this line of reasoning be developed dramatically as well as philosophically, and the end result could not have been so cogent and persuasive except for the incarnation of these philosophical concerns within the structure of a human drama. Albert Camus, not unlike many of today's thinkers, feels that the serious problems and choices that face us are not to be met through the meditation of a rational scheme, but only through a lucid and obstinate attention to the fleeting picture of human existence.

CHAPTER IV

A LAST WORD ABOUT
THE ABSURD

WE HAVE followed the "few familiar ideas" of the thought of Albert Camus, and we have seen them "polished" and "transformed" during a decade of peace, war, occupation, and liberation. These few ideas which Camus calls his own are those which spring from solitude. The general mode in which these ideas are expressed is in the relation between man, as an individual, and the universe. And within this context Camus has maintained that, from the point of view of our immediate personal experience, this relation is characterized by absurdity. Camus feels that the absurdity of this relation is demonstrated by two undeniable elements in human experience, i.e., (1) the strange, inhuman flux of the universe in face of our desire for a unified and familiar universe and (2) the destiny of total death which can be neither escaped nor understood. Man, the world, and the Absurd: these are the concerns of the early phase of the thought of Albert Camus.

In our analysis of the thought of Camus it has been seen that from *Noces* there is a direct movement into the problems of *The Stranger*, and that, subsequently, *The Myth of Sisyphus* and the two plays are an aberration from the problems as first set forth, this aberration being justified as an experiment in absurdist reasoning. This experiment can only be seen as an aberration, because it draws logical consequences from the premise of the total absurdity of the universe, a premise which is not present in *Noces* or *The Stranger*. In the latter two works the awareness of death and of the inhuman character of the world does not negate the beauty and fascination which the world has for human experience. However, in *The Myth* and in *The Misunderstanding* this partial absurdity has been absolutized, making the world itself a threat to the dignity of man. The play, *Caligula*, is a demonstration that the absurdist experiment has been pushed to its terrible limits, and that the authentic concerns in the philosophy of Albert Camus have once again been taken up.

What must be clearly understood, however, is that the reappearance of the original themes of Camus' thought does not mean that these themes have suffered no transformation. Man's relation to the world is viewed in a new light because of the results of the absurdist experiment. The passive estrangement which man suffered in face of the Absurd is now no longer passive. It is active and agressive. The *raisonnement absurde* has brought us to a new clarity in which we know that, even though this world is without God or fixed values, it does possess limits. Man in his relation to the world does not have unlimited freedom; everything is not permissible. The unbridled development of the consequences of the absurd experience has, in the end, given rise to an essential dimension of human experience which opposes and supercedes the Absurd. This dimension is revolt. After the encounter with revolt the original themes of Camus' thought find themselves transformed and emended.

Not only can the philosophy of Albert Camus be considered in two separate phases, but even within this first period there is a constant shifting, exploration, and development of ideas which are shaped by the shifting character of human experience itself. Interpreters of the thought of Albert Camus have generally distinguished between the stages of *l'absurde* and *la révolte*, but from the analysis we have made it should be apparent that this early stage cannot be taken *en bloc*, philosophically, because of the contradictory stages within it. Nor does it seem that a literary analysis alone could discover this continual development of thought. Camus is a writer who is motivated by serious philosophical concerns; without recognition and study of these philosophical concerns we can understant neither his literary efforts nor the many moments of his developing philosophy. We have already indicated how Sartre attempts to assess *The Stranger* strictly in terms of the essays of *The Myth of Sisyphus*, only to confound the proper structure of the novel. Camus suffers this same injustice at the hands of other commentators.[1] A more general misunderstanding of the thought of Albert Camus is that which attempts to lump together the ideas of *Noces* with those which finally emerge from the absurdist experiment. In the case of Michel Mohrt, Camus is seen as a poet, somewhat on the order of Rimbaud or Tzara, who lives in a wild and sensual anarchy and whose revolt is "against physical ills, against death" but at the same time has the "temptation to say yea to the world, to take one's ease in this comradely creation."[2] For Mohrt, these are "the two complementary reactions of a single body of thought, face to face with the absurdity of existence."[3] Mohrt views Camus in the same way that Camus had spoken of the naïve worldliness of his fellow Algerians, and a revolt against physical ills and death is the natural and unthinking revolt of the purely sensual person. But this ignores the absurdist experiment, during which we saw man's revolt against the world to be based on a demand for unity and coherence. This intellectual basis for man's accusation of the world is essential to Camus' thought. And it is not simply "ease" which is desired; it is order and meaning in the world. Nothing could be so damaging to the thought of Albert Camus than to mark him as a sensualist whose concerns are poetic and not philosophical. His works are partially incomprehensible without their philosophical structure, and it is not surprising that a poetical approach to his works ends in a distorted picture of the man.

A more interesting estimation of this early phase of Camus' thought is that of Manuel de Dièguez.[4] Dièguez points out what he sees as an inconsistency in the thought of Albert

Camus, to-wit, if, in *The Myth of Sisyphus*, Camus affirms the nihilistic formula, "tout est permis," then by what right can Sisyphus, or Kirolov, or Meursault say "tout est bien"? This critic believes that in the absurd myth itself the hero has broken through absurdity into a world of value. Although Dièguez makes the mistake of other commentators in taking all of the works of this first period *en bloc*, still the value of his comment is that it indicates that even within the absurdist experiment itself Camus could not completely negate man's dependence on the beauty of the world. After having insisted on the necessity of maintaining the absurd confrontation, Camus seems to present Sisyphus as having given in to the absurdity of life and yet found happiness therein. Looking back at this period of his thought Camus himself might now admit that his experiment was not completely "controlled."

The *raisonnement absurde*, which constitutes the most venturesome philosophical work of Camus' early thought, is a courageous and surprising effort. Camus puts it forth, cognizant of the untenable character of the results which his radical method has produced. This type of experimental philosophy is unprecedented and serves to emphasize the peculiar role which Camus conceives to be that of the modern philosopher. But for a man who has made an unqualified rejection of rational-systematic thought this seems to be the only honest approach to the questions of our times. Camus' approach is that of analytical explorations of giving problems in human experience. This means that philosophizing finds its proper form in the essay, and it is just to say that Camus has never gone beyond the bounds of the essay style. Even the extensive *L'Homme révolté* is actually a group of related essays; it is not a systematic work. Albert Camus obviously has these things in mind when he insists that he is not a philosopher. By this he means that he does not proceed through induction to construct a rationally consistent picture of our universe. He can only proceed by analytical and deductive methods with what he feels are given realities of human experience; when the analysis has reached its terminus, there it remains; there is no possibility of merging the structure of the essay into a larger interpretive scheme. Albert Camus is an essayist and moral philosopher, and thus stands within a long tradition of French philosophers. His early concern with the themes of existentialist thought should not obscure this fact; certainly, his most recent writings, since *L'Homme révolté*, should convince us that his concerns are not those of existentialism. He stands out as a modern humanist; this much one can say. Whether or not he is an atheistic humanist is a judgment which, it seems to us, cannot be made, despite the strictly non-theistic direction of his thought. When, in his essays, it appears that he is suggesting an atheistic position, Camus has inserted footnote references to caution that he is not making such an inference. Because of his bent to philosophize in essay form, we will know whether Camus is an atheist only when he writes an essay on God; it is unlikely that this will ever come to pass.

The experience of the Absurd is certainly a dominant philosophical problem of our times. In its genesis it is not a speculative problem but a human experience. The peculiarly subjective character of this experience has set the pattern for an anti-rationalistic attitude among those philosophers who have made this their central interest. If this anguish, nausea, or absurdity constitutes a basic, given concern for existential thought, then it is incredible, in the eyes of Albert Camus, that the foremost philosophers of the Absurd should not have followed this given truth into the realm of moral philosophy. Instead, they have not "held to" the notion of the Absurd. These men have explored the human anguish which seems consequent of the discovery of the fragmentation and unknowability of our universe and have ended by either accepting this as ultimate or by negating it through an affirmation of transcendent unity. Camus has taken the position that if this vision of absurdity is true, then our task is to analyze it and deduce from it the obvious consequences for human conduct. Camus not only reproaches the "existentialists" for not taking seriously their essential problem, but also for not having sufficiently examined the nature of the absurd experience. To do so, he maintains, is to understand that the feeling of the absurdity of the universe is possible only if we as human beings possess some standard or need which contradicts what we find in the universe. The experience of an absurd universe does not mean the total absurdity of human existence. The very experience of the Absurd is possible only because of a contradiction, of a divorce between human requisites and the clear indifference of the world. Hence, this experience is a moment of lucidity when we are aware of the essential divorce between human nature and the creation in which it is placed. We must note that here in the heart of his absurdist experiment Camus founds the position that there is a human nature. This is not an existence which must remain chartless for man; the experience of the Absurd is the proof of man's uniqueness and the foundation of his dignity and freedom. Caligula has made the mistake of acting as if human existence were a total absurdity; it is inevitable that he should be destroyed by a revolt which is the social expression of that same human vindication of itself that is expressed in the absurd experience. Having discovered a uniqueness in man which rejects the irrationality of the world, we have now found that this same unique nature rejects and revolts against certain conditions in human society. Out of this analysis of the absurd experience Camus has brought a concept of man which becomes the basis for a moral philosophy capable now of a positive attack on the ethical-political problems of the twentieth century.

At the same time Camus has rejected those consequences of the Absurd which are the issue of the solitary confrontation of man and the universe, to the exclusion of man's social involvement. When the social dimension is included, then we find that our freedom is not boundless, nor the quantity of experience the only "morality." This solitary anguish of absurdity has been relentlessly drawn out to its proper consequences, and these consequences are found to be insufficient for a moral philosophy because of the exclusion of the social dimension. Thus, Albert Camus appears to have given the last word on the problem of the Absurd which has so fascinated existential thought. In his *Process and Reality*,[5] Alfred N. Whitehead has made the observation that in the history of philosophy there has always been the man who founds a philosophical tradition but has not clarified all of its terms, and that there is the man who so integrates the terms of that philosophy that its inadequacy is brought to light. Albert Camus stands in some such terminal relation to the philosophy of the Absurd. But if he be the Hume who has shown the insufficiency of this line of thought, he stands also as the Kant who, in the philosophy of revolt, has once more brought us into a hopeful and positive relation with the creation and its creatures.

Camus himself has made clear the transition which takes place between the absurdist experiment and the later positive philosophy of revolt, i.e.,

At least here we have the first bit of progress that the spirit of revolt brings to bear on a reflection which was first penetrated with absurdity and the apparent sterility of the world. In the absurd experience the tragedy is individual. With the movement of revolt it is conscious of being collective. It is the adventure of all. The first progress of a mind struck by this estrangement [*étrangeté*] is to recognize that he shares this estranged condition with all men, and that human reality in its totality suffers from this distance in the relation of oneself and the world.[6]

In regard to the insufficiency of the Absurd as a guide for human action, he affirms that

". . . the absurd is contradictory in existence. It excludes judgments of value and judgments of value *are*. They are, because they are bound to the very fact of existing. It is necessary then to replace the absurdist line of reasoning by its equivalent in existence which is revolt.[7]

Of course, even though we can sympathize with this transition from the solipsism of the Absurd to the community of revolt, still we cannot allow Camus to abandon one position for another without some reproach. For it is true that despite the "experimental" character of Camus' absurdist thought, there is no denying the passionate manner in which Camus gave himself to this experiment. Camus cannot disclaim a *"parti pris"* in *The Myth of Sisyphus*. That this is so is seen in two later remarks that reveal the abandonment of his earlier attitude. The first is in a passing reference later made to "the dark walls *(murs obscurs)* against which we feel our way, the yet invisible places where the gates may open."[8] Having used the same metaphor, "walls," which he had employed in *The Myth of Sisyphus* as the "absurd walls" *(murs absurdes)* to describe the universe about us, this distinction between absurdity and darkness is indicative of the abandonment of the early solipsism. More conclusive, in this respect, is a remark made by Camus during an interview in 1951. Having been asked a question relative to *The Myth of Sisyphus*, Camus begins his answer with the statement, "J'étais alors plus pessimiste que je ne suis."[9]

The clearest explanation put forth by Camus as to the nature of this transition in his philosophy is found in the Introduction to *L'Homme révolté*. This introduction is the hinge between the early and later philosophy of Albert Camus. It is not so much an introduction to *L'Homme révolté* as it is a conclusion to his *raisonnement absurde*, and without knowledge of the latter, the reader might find this introduction incomprehensible. Camus best justifies the transition in his thought with the following statement, i.e.,

Nothing remains in the absurdist attitude which can help us answer the questions of our time. The absurdist method, like that

70

of systematic doubt, has wiped the slate clean. It leaves us in a blind alley. But, like the method of doubt, it can, by returning upon itself, disclose a new field of investigation. Reasoning follows the same reflexive course. I proclaim that I believe in nothing and that everything is absurd, but I cannot doubt the validity of my own proclamation and I am compelled to believe, at least, in my own protest. The first, and only, datum that is furnished me, within absurdist experience, is rebellion. Stripped of all knowledge, driven to commit murder or consent to it, I possess this single datum which gains greater strength from the anguish that I suffer. Rebellion arises from the spectacle of the irrational coupled with an unjust and incomprehensible condition. But its blind impetus clamours for order in the midst of chaos, and for unity in the very heart of the ephemeral.[10]

The developing philosophy of Albert Camus shows Camus as an example of his own estimate of the nature of man, to-wit, "Man is the only creature who refuses to be what he is."[11]

of systematic doubt, has wiped the slate clean. It leaves us in a blind alley. But, like the method of doubt, it can, by returning upon itself, disclose a new field of investigation. Reasoning follows the same reflexive course. I proclaim that I believe in nothing and that everything is absurd, but I cannot doubt the validity of my own proclamation and I am compelled to believe, at least, in my own protest. The first, and only, datum that is furnished me, within absurdist experience, is rebellion. Stripped of all knowledge, driven to commit murder or consent to it, I possess this single datum which gains greater strength from the anguish that I suffer. Rebellion arises from the spectacle of the irrational coupled with an unjust and incomprehensible condition. But its blind impetus clamours for order in the midst of chaos, and for unity in the very heart of the ephemeral."

The developing philosophy of Albert Camus shows Camus as an example of his own estimate of the nature of man, to-wit, "Man is the only creature who refuses to be what he is."

PART TWO:

MAN, THE WORLD,

AND MEN: REVOLT

CHAPTER V
REVOLT AND VALUE

In 1945 Albert Camus published an essay entitled *"Remarque sur la révolte."*[1] It was included in a collection of essays edited by his friend and former professor in Alger, Jean Grenier. This short essay, which is roughly the same as that which opens *L'Homme révolté*, is an interpretive analysis of the human experience of revolt. In this anatomy of revolt Camus has presented a definition of terms for what we shall call a "philosophy of revolt." This philosophy begins with the analysis of a given human experience, even as the absurdist experiment began with an analysis of the experience of absurdity. With the direction of his thought here defined, Camus developed these concepts over the following five years in his journalistic work and in 1951 presented *L'Homme révolté*.

What is happening when a man revolts? In revolt, says Camus, a man is saying not only "no," but also "yes." By his "no" he is defining a limit and frontier, and by his "yes" he is affirming all that is within that frontier. In revolt a man feels that he is right and the oppressor is wrong. The rebel refuses either that he should do a certain thing or else that a certain thing should be done to him. Hence, in revolting, a man affirms something irreducible within him, i.e., a value. To the measure that patience is exhausted, this value defines itself more and more strongly until, in revolt, it emerges as a total demand. What was previously only a part of man now becomes his total being, and he demands all or nothing for this value, which is to say that this value is worth the risk of death. That the rebel will die for this value means that the value is more general than his own individuality. Revolt is not egocentric, for a man may revolt against the general social conditions in which he lives. Moreover, revolt may come from the unoppressed who has identified his destiny with that of the oppressed. Hence, revolt affirms the complicity of all men around a common value and against a common oppression. It affirms a value which all men possess, even the oppressor himself. It carries man toward all men, showing that the solidarity of men is metaphysical, or, as Camus puts it, that this value is "horizontally transcendent" of the individual.

This passion for man as man, evoked by revolt, is not to be confused with a passion for an ideal man as is seen in the thought of Scheller, Rousseau, or Bentham; this is the passion of Nietzsche, or Heathcliff, or Ivan Karamazov who rejected the order of God for that of man. The positive human value that has been revealed shows us that revolt is to human experience what the *cogito* is to thought. It is a primal truth, creative of a primal value.

Revolt, as it is here understood, is a phenomenon of Western civilization. This is because it is conditioned in a society in which there is a theoretical equality in contradiction with an actual inequality. Camus expands this observation by stating that for the human spirit there are but two possible universes, i.e., that of revolt or that of the sacred or, in Christian terms, grace. In the Hindu world, for example, the tradition is sacred, and there is no possibility of a metaphysical problem arising. Metaphysics has been replaced by myth; there are no questions because all answers have been given once and for all time. But once the world is no longer sacred and the eternal responses are forgotten or rejected, then man demands a human order in which all the responses are humanly justifiable. This movement of whole societies from the sacred toward the world of revolt is an historical phenomenon, thus revealing the metaphysical problem of revolt as existent on an historical scale. But the apparent relativity of the phenomenon of revolt does not mean that it is not integral with human existence.

To say that the problem is relative to the epoch is not at all to say that it is not primary in man and that it has value only in the framework of an individualistic morality. To the contrary, it is to say that the epoch, by virtue of its conflict, has brought to the fore one of the essential dimensions of man. It is an authentic value, which is to say, a motive for action, which is thus furnished us by revolt.[2]

Camus is concerned that a clear distinction be made between revolt and revolution. The latter involves the translation of a clear idea into history; it is the attempt to bring history completely into accord with a theoretical plan of stability. Revolt, to the contrary begins with human experience and moves toward an indefinite but imperative idea. Hence, revolution, involving as it does a clear idea, should be a complete turnover in which society receives a definite and complete stability. But in fact, this definitive revolution neither has nor will ever take place. When the movement of the revolutionary idea seems to have come full circle in its incarnation into history, the historical situation has moved beyond that which was originally envisaged by the revolutionary idea; thus, the definitive revolution does not take place, and a new revolution is needed to attempt once more the completion of the circle. Camus here shows his affinity to the Ephesian philosopher who had said "You cannot step into the same river twice." Since the 19th century we have not had revolutions but only the progressive and ever incomplete affirmation by man of himself.

In revolt as well as in revolution, there is a demand for freedom and justice. But in the historical event of revolution freedom will always come into conflict with the demand for justice, or *vice-versa*, thus giving rise to a new revolt and a new affirmation by man of himself. Revolution not only differs with but comes into conflict with the more basic movement of revolt. It is for this reason that revolutions fail if they negate the complicity and solidarity of men which revolt had revealed. Solidarity is negated when, through violence and political realism, falsehood and silence become the structure of society. Already, the value found by revolt shows its conflicts with other actions; the solidarity of men cannot survive in a world where silence is imposed between men and buttressed with falsehood. And Camus sees a direct link between hatred and falsehood, as seen in the following remark:

Hatred can use no other mask, it cannot do without this weapon. One cannot hate without lying. And, inversely, one cannot speak the truth without replacing hatred with understanding. Nine-tenths of the newspapers in the world today lie, to a greater or lesser extent. This is because they are, in differing degrees, spokesmen for hatred and blindness. The greater their hatred, the more they lie.[3]

The active complicity of men is the value born in revolt. This complicity is able to survive in face of an absurd world, but it cannot live in silence and falsehood. Complicity may be lost also because of pretensions to absoluteness in a revolution, whether this be in the attempt to establish absolute justice or absolute freedom. In either case, the irreducible part of man is oppressed. According to Camus, the value of human complicity can be maintained only in the relative, and any revolution which is faithful to the human condition must seek no more than a relative or proximate stability. Within this relative condition the effort must be made to strengthen the solidarity of men. This is the ongoing task which moves toward the perfection of a total complicity of men; this, in ideal terms, is what would constitute a definitive revolution.

By way of review we may say that any man who revolts puts to the fore two terms: the power, regime, or man who oppresses him and the value within him which he affirms and defends. Holding to his evidence, i.e., given human experience, Camus finds that, in general, we may say that one revolts against the human condition and affirms a value. One says "yes" to the complicity of men and "no" to the condition of men. This is a tautology in constant movement: in the same instant in which the irreducible part of man is affirmed, there is recognition of the threat under which it lies. In revolt, the human condition is simultaneously affirmed and called into question. Thus, neither term of the revolt can be affirmed absolutely and irrevocably, and, in order to exist, human revolt must be ceaselessly reaffirmed and sustained in tension. It is clear then that Albert Camus has not outlined a sociological problem, but has presented us with an analysis of "an essential dimension of human experience." We cannot speak of this as the "concept" or "principle" of revolt, for revolt is not an intellectual product; it is a human experience and action. And within this experience Camus finds an "essential dimension," because revolt is creative of a value, is a judgment of one's condition and is a motive for action. In revolt, man is intensely conscious of what he is and of what the world is, and in this clarifying movement he realizes his complicity with all men who share this condition, whether in the consciousness of revolt or not. The rebel is still within a closed universe, and revolt has not taught him anything which negates the "Absurd," but what he does know is that through revolt he can, without help of the eternal, create his own values. Revolt begins with and carries man beyond the anguish which is the terminus of existential thought. Revolt is a course of action which is beyond both human anguish and the illusion of eternity.

The further clarification of revolt and its value is not a task for rational speculation. Revolt is a human experience whose content is to be probed not within a rational structure set up by the mind; it can be explored only through observation of its appearances in human history. As Camus has remarked elsewhere, "Philosophy is action"; its analytical function is bound to the movement of history. "A philosophical examination of revolutions should then help us to state precisely the content of a value revealed by the movement of revolt."[4] This, of course, was the purpose of *L'Homme révolté*, Camus' most comprehensive work up to this point.

These analytical essays on revolt, it should be observed, show a great likeness to the way in which Camus had formerly analyzed the experience of the Absurd and then proceeded to examine the manner in which other thinkers had treated this notion. Here, even as in the *raisonnement absurde*, Camus specifies a rule of method which is to guide us in an examination of the history of revolt; a method which is ordained by the essential nature of revolt and which can enable us to judge whether revolt is "held to" or is betrayed in its historical revolutionary manifestations. To begin with, we have the value of complicity to hold to

. . . but, let us note before going ahead, the foundation of this value is revolt itself. The solidarity of men is founded on the movement of revolt which, in its turn, finds its justification only in this complicity. We shall, then, have the right to say that all revolt which denies or destroys this solidarity, loses at the same moment the name of revolt and actually coincides with a murderous consentment. In the same way, this solidarity, separated from the sacred, takes life only on the level of revolt. The true drama of rebel thought is thus announced. In order to be, man must revolt, but his revolt must respect the limit that it reveals in itself and where men, joining themselves with it, begin to be. Rebel thought cannot do without memory: it is a perpetual tension. In following it in its works and in its acts, we shall be able to say each time if it remains faithful to its original nobility, or if, through weariness and madness, it forgets it in a drunkenness of tyranny or slavery.[5]

Man must revolt in order to be. This is what Camus means when he says that revolt is to human experience what the *cogito* is to thought. The formula is, "I revolt, therefore we are."[6]

CHAPTER VI
REVOLT IN HISTORY

FROM an historical perspective the phenomenon of revolt in the modern occidental world is to be viewed under two rubrics, namely, that of metaphysical revolt and, secondly, that of historical revolt. Metaphysical revolt is man's protest against his own condition as well as all creation; it is metaphysical because its protest concerns the ultimate ends of man and of creation. Camus contrasts this with historical revolt in which the oppressed and enslaved man, while recognizing the metaphysical conditions of his existence, protests against that immediate situation which oppresses him and behind which there is a master, a regime, or some accountable power. In either case, whether the protest be against the general or the immediate condition of life, man founds his revolt on a dimly perceived value within himself. Camus considers the conscious efforts of modern man to transform society through revolutionary action as examples of historical revolt. Metaphysical revolt comprises those modern philosophical and literary revolts against heaven itself which are characterized not so much by atheism as by a complete defiance of God. Camus has offered a valuable category for philosophical classification which cuts across the terms "modern," "existential," and "Marxist." The metaphysical revolts as well as the historical revolts share the common source of the recognized solidarity of men. The task is to ascertain the fidelity which these expressions of revolt have had to their origins.

METAPHYSICAL REVOLT

Metaphysical revolt finds its beginning during the latter

decades of the 18th century, but Camus finds that there are at least five ancient prototypes for this type of revolt. Prometheus stands as the first great hero to revolt against the gods, and Achilles is another mythological figure in revolt. There is also Plato's Callicles, Lucretius, and Epicurus who take the part of man in their defiance of God. But the fiercest kind of revolt and the type which is nearest to our own, says Camus, is that which is directed against a personal god. With the development of the consciousness of a personal god, man becomes accountable for his actions in a direct relation to his god; the notion of crime is born. Hence, Cain is more representative of modern metaphysical revolt than are these antique heroes. For the progeny of Cain, evil and death were the reasons for their revolt against the jealous God of Abraham. This rift between the omnipotent and jealous Jehovah and man was to be closed in the Christ. Christ, the god-man, took upon himself the suffering and death which are the lot of men and, to the last, did not avail himself of the privileges of divinity. Without resource in his agony, Christ was God completely subjected to the human condition, and thus the rift was closed between God and man. If God himself had freely suffered the condition of men, then man himself could no longer revolt against the lot which was his. This was the triumph of Christianity, but with the advent of an age of critical reason the divinity of the man, Jesus, was denied, and man found himself once again alone and without solace in his misery. The rift reappeared, and Jesus was acclaimed as an innocent, sharing wholly in the human condition and marking merely another milestone in the history of its suffering. As before, the heavens hovered above mankind, implacable and silent, and the preparations were complete for the metaphysical revolt of our times.

The Marquis de Sade is, according to Camus, the first great rebel to launch an assault against heaven. In Sade we find a revolt which is furious and unbridled; it is a revolt which roars out an absolute negation and demands a monstrous freedom. His twenty-seven years in prison severed his fury from reality and channeled it into a dream which had but one logic: that of feeling. In Sade we find the reasoning, which is shared as well by Camus, that if there is a God and He permits the injustice and suffering that we see on earth then this God is a criminal deity who denies and murders. If God, Himself, denies man justice and morality, then why should not man do the same? Upon these grounds, Sade not only denies all human order and ethics but denies God as well, and this on the basis of what he feels is the most immediate and exigent power in man, i.e., the sexual instinct. It is to a force of nature that Sade clings in his rebellion against the order of heaven and earth, and it is this force which is the matrix of his thought. The liberty which Sade demanded was not a liberty of principles but of instincts; liberty is not his actual goal, but rather libertinism. Following his logic of passion Sade denies that virtue can exist in a life of freedom. The only principle which Sade can draw from his frenzy is that of a will power with its desire for destruction and domination.

The value of Sade for a study of revolt is that he shows the extreme consequences of the logic of revolt when, through a pent up and demented fury, the origins of this revolt are forgotten. We find in Sade much which is contemporary with our present age, e.g.,

the demand for total freedom and the process of dehumanization coldly exercised by the intellect. The reduction of man to an experimental object, the ordering which specifies the relations between the will to power and the man-object, the enclosed arena of this monstrous experiment, are the lessons which the theorists of power will refind when they are to organize the age of slavery.[1]

At this early period, Sade has exalted the totalitarian society in the name of a furious liberty which betrays the limits set by true revolt. In the Marquis there "truly begins contemporary history and tragedy."[2]

In romanticism Camus finds another aspect of the metaphysical revolt which resembles that of Sade in its stress on defiance and refusal without the necessary concomitant emphasis on the value which is born in revolt. Romanticism finds its heroes among those who defy the moral and divine laws, but whose expression of this is in out-lawry and unconventionality. The hero of romanticism is not the revolutionary but the dandy. Defying the laws of God, the dandy has created his own coherence and law by becoming a *personnage*, a "character." What the dandy feels most poignantly is his own solitude and individuality, and his eccentricity and non-conformity is the method through which he gains a public that mirrors his own existence, thereby reassuring him of a certain marginal solidarity with the society of men. His denial of God and a divine order in society, forces him, as a point of honor, to break with the conventional life of men, but this break comes only in a superficial demonstration of his independence and revolt, which is superficial precisely because he fears a complete break with society. Thus, there is a lack of positive content in the revolt of the dandys, a confusion of good and evil from which they cannot emerge. Their realm is that of solitude, engaged in a lonely creativity which rivals that of God: this is an esthetic which is still powerful today. But within romanticism itself there has been the movement gradually away from the world of appearance to the 20th century world of action, which has also been a movement away from the original solitude toward a reunion with men. Romanticism, in this respect, moves toward the time of social revolution and is faithful to its origins. But along with this emerging social revolutionary drive there came the taste for frenzy and for apocalypticism which was to pervert the demands of the revolt.

In his discussion of the metaphysical revolts, Camus is most interested in the contributions made to this movement by Dostoievski and Nietzsche. In the case of Sade and the romantics there is a revolt in which the "no" is stressed to the exclusion of an affirmation of that value which authorizes the revolt. But in Dostoievski we find a groping for the value which supports man's defiance of God. In Nietzsche there is a progress which takes revolt out of its indeterminacy and makes a positive affirmation of human values that are all-sufficing.

Dostoievski's most eloquent spokesman for the metaphysical revolt is Ivan Karamazov. In Ivan, Albert Camus has also found his own spokesman, and one whose ideas echo through almost all of Camus' works. The dandys did not go so far as to refuse God; they raised themselves to a level of equality and defiance of Him. Ivan goes farther than this: he refuses God in the name of a superior value: justice. Rebel thought has arrived at a new stage when the rebel judges and condemns God in the name of a value which is higher than either God or man. Ivan revolts against God and the Christian faith because this faith links human suffering with truth, and innocent death with true faith. Suffering and innocent death are unjust and no mystification can obscure this. "All the science in the world is not worth the tears of children," says Ivan. God's mysterious love and immortality are offered as salvation, but even if this salvation were possible Ivan would refuse it in the name of human justice. It is this "even if" that marks a new stage in the history of rebel thought; Ivan refuses salvation for the sake of the imperative truth of justice.

The "all or nothing" that the rebel demands for his value becomes, in the case of Ivan, a demand that justice be for everyone or no one. Even though it were possible that he could be saved, still Ivan realizes that others would be damned and that suffering would continue among men. If all men cannot be saved, then he will not be saved alone; the demand for justice is inseparable from the rebel's solidarity with all men, and if all cannot find salvation, then this is clearly an injustice. In refusing salvation, Ivan rejects the meaning and order which faith and immortality give to human existence; even so, Ivan prefers to remain earth-bound, "not knowing why," and faithful to the value which he understands. But the rejection of immortality entails a denial of ultimate reward and punishment and hence the denial of any final good or evil. If there be no ultimate good or evil in human existence, then both virtue and law are meaningless: everything is permitted. In romanticism, everything is not permitted; only insolence was allowed as the proof of one's protest. But Ivan, in his revolt against evil and death, has carried his protest into a hopeless negation of all order in life and is delivered into nihilism.

The question which Ivan finally poses, that which constitutes the true progress which Dostoievski brings about in the spirit of revolt, is the only one which interests us here: can one live and maintain one's self in revolt?

Ivan allows us to guess his reply: one can live in revolt only by pushing it all the way to the end. What is the extreme end of the metaphysical revolt? The metaphysical revolution. The master of this world, after having his legitimacy contested, should be overthrown. Man should take his place. "Since God and immortality do not exist, the new man is permitted to become God." But what does it mean to be God? Simply to recognize that everything is permitted; to refuse every other law except one's own.[3]

Ivan pushes his revolt all the way to the end and there finds madness. "Caught between an unjustifiable virtue and an inacceptable crime, devoured with pity and incapable of love, a solitary man deprived of a saving cynicism, contradiction will kill this sovereign intellect."[4]

The metaphysical revolt has now moved into action; it has broken into the moral and social field. But it breaks into action with principles, "everything is permitted" and "everyone or no one," and upon these seeks to remake creation for the sake of the divinity of men. Nihilism has now become a political principle with unforeseeable consequences. The legend of the Grand Inquisitor is nothing but a projection of these nihilistic principles into a possible mode of action. If everything is permitted and the world is to be remade without God, then the Grand Inquisitor is justified in attempting to unite mankind through a reign of death and destruction. The revolt of Ivan ended in madness, but the extreme consequences of his revolt remained: consequences which in their bitter defiance of God lead to the frenetic effort to create a world of absolute unity and absolute justice by any means, including injustice itself. Ivan, as well as Sade, has prepared the way for the coming of Caesar.

Ivan's refusal of salvation moved into an absurdity from which it could not emerge. Although God is denied in the name of a moral value, how can such a value be understood without God? Ivan has, in effect, opposed one God to another. The absurdity of this position is to be surpassed only by denying morality as being a vestige of the old belief in God. There are not two Gods but merely one, whose power is effete but not yet totally destroyed. It remained for Nietzsche to supply the *coup de grace*. Camus points out that Nietzsche's older contemporary, Stirner, took the step of denying both God and morality but was content to remain within this nihilism. Stirner affirmed all that was unique in the individual in complete defiance of anything which thwarts or attacks this uniqueness, whether it be God, the state, society, or "humanity." Man's only liberty is in personal power, his one truth is an isolated egoism, his one good is that which he can use. Stirner so completely affirms the free sovereignty of the individual that all existing outside the individual is an enemy to him. This being so, there are no crimes, faults, or sin; to live means to transgress and to assert one's uniqueness. To accept this role man must realize the criminality of his uniqueness, which means that murder is legitimatized. In Stirner's extreme nihilistic revolt Camus finds there is only death or resurrection, nothing more. Revolt has here issued in a drunkenness of destruction in which the solidarity of men no longer finds its place. Nihilistic revolt leads into a desert of solitude; a desert from which Nietzsche emerges with a renaissance of man's faith in life. Fidelity to one's revolt demands that nihilism be surpassed.

Friedrich Nietzsche accepted the nihilism of his times and asked whether one could actually live without believing anything. His answer was yes, provided we methodically push our negation to its limits. Camus feels that Nietzsche's was a methodical revolt, an undeniable prophetism which was controlled by his own analysis of the *malaise* of the 19th century.

It is Nietzsche as a clinician whom we must clearly understand before accepting his prophetism. In his analytical thinking, Nietzsche begins with and ends in atheism, which for man means that there is neither unity nor finality in the universe. This being so, the *is* of the world cannot be criticised by a supposed *ought*. If there be no God then there is no oughtness in the world, and, hence, value judgments are impossible. Idealistic morality is attacked by Nietzsche because it denies the *is* and the flesh, and takes refuge in reflection which negates this world. God being dead, the only true morality is that which lucidly affirms what is. Idealism's denial of the world is essentially immoral. In attacking God and the Christian faith, Nietzsche had as his object the moral nature of this religion. Nietzsche's estimate of Jesus of Nazareth was that he proclaimed a message of works and of assent to the confusion of good and evil in the world. It was the Church which had corrupted this message with the introduction of the ideas of judgment, punishment, and reward, thus transforming the real ends of history in terms of supposed ideal ends. Camus has in mind here the later period of Nietzsche's thought, especially that of *The Will to Power*. He notes that Nietzsche attacks socialism for the same reasons, to wit, that socialism places a reward and punishment concept at the end of history and envisions the proletariat as moving toward a collective messianism. But the bulwark of this denial of the world is the Church, whose message he terms as one of "nihilism," meaning by this a doctrine which negates the reality of this world.

In his role of clinician, Nietzsche's great discovery, in the eyes of Camus, was that true freedom can be founded only upon a law. It is in this discovery that rebel thought emerges from nihilism. If the rebel finds that nothing is true, this does not authorize him to act as if everything is permitted. If nothing is true, then, says Nietzsche, *nothing is permitted*. This is to say that complete freedom can only entail complete bondage; unless we know what is possible and what is forbidden we cannot act. If man breaks the tablets of the old laws he is obliged to create new laws before he will find freedom. God's death, then, solves nothing. Now, man has the task of creating new laws and values in the light of his discovery that the earth is our one truth and the place where salvation will be found. Such a task requires a superhuman effort and will be wrought in the extremity of man's solitude.

The creative efforts of man take place in a world of becoming which has no end. To fulfill our superhuman task we must accept our own fatality with joy and give ourselves wholly to the endless becoming of the world, an act in which our individuality is lost within the world's eternal movement. Camus emphasizes the significance of Nietzsche's attempt to prove that there is a law in the eternal becoming of the world. For Nietzsche, the world is God to whom we say "yes" and in whose divinity we participate. This world is gratuitous and is incapable of being comprehended by any human judgment. Only art renders proper homage to the world, precisely because it is a repetition and not a recreation. This is the Hellenic esthetics which Camus shared with Nietzsche in the early period of his thought, but which is rejected, as we shall see later, in his esthetics of revolt.

In deifying the world, Nietzsche has found a God which is a Creator and no longer a Judge. Man's part is to accept what is in this world with respect and with passion. In Camus' estimate, the Nietzschean injunction for man to throw himself into the cosmos in order to participate in its divinity is a leap and risk, not differing from that proposed by Pascal or by the Christian faith in general.

The enormous historic corruption of Nietzsche's thought in Nazism comes from the fact that his prophetic message of the superman was severed from his analysis of nihilism out of which the prophecy sprang. If the "clinical" aspect of Nietzcheanism is ignored, then the "yes" which one says to all human experience applies to murder as well. The "yes" of the slave, like that of Jesus, accepts the suffering that is man's lot, but the "yes" of the master is an affirmation of the system of slavery—a categorically different affirmation. Nietzsche's contribution to the metaphysical revolt was that he moved from the simple negation of the ideal to its secularization. Salvation no longer coming from God, man must give himself to the eternal becoming of the world and there make his salvation. But Nietzsche nevertheless contributed to the battle for empire of the 20th century. Disregarding his analytical thought, socialism adopted his originally individualistic doctrines of the will to power and the superman, doctrines which find their union with that of the classless society in Marxist-Leninism. Camus makes the interesting comparison of Marx to Nietzsche as that of a Christian to a Greek, i.e., Marx desires to subjugate nature for the sake of history, whereas Nietzsche desires to use nature to conquer history.[5] In any case, much of Nietzsche's philosophy was absorbed into Leninism, and the nihilism which Nietzsche sought to surpass has become consecrated.

If the final outcome of the great movement of revolt in the 19th and 20th centuries is this pitiless enslavement, must not one turn his back to revolt and once more take up Nietzche's desperate cry to his epoch: 'My conscience and yours are no longer the same conscience'?[6]

Freed from the shackles of God, rebellious man now turns to find himself imprisoned within reason and history.

The last instance of metaphysical revolt treated by Camus is the poetic revolt of Lautréamont, Rimbaud, and the surrealists, a revolt more abortive than successful, primarily because of its vacillation between a concern for the world of appearances and that of action. In surrealism we see the attempt to find rule and order within irrationality and insanity. In the case of Lautréamont the expression of revolt is not greatly different from that of romanticism, but Lautréamont is so impressed by the ultimate uselessness of his revolt that he condemns everything, including man. His is a "convulsive attempt" to evade God, the world, and man, but the extreme evil of this attempt convinces him that his revolt must be false. Lautréamont finds his refuge in a radical banality and conventionality, in which man remains an agnostic but does his duty toward society. At least we learn from Lautréamont that "conformity is one of the nihilistic temptations of revolt which dominates a large part of our intellectual history. In any case, it shows how the rebel who engages in action, if he forgets his origins, is tempted by the greatest conformity."[7]

Rimbaud, who is the source for the surrealist movement, is, to Camus, the greatest poet of revolt. But this greatness finds its expression only in his works and not in his life. The influence of Rimbaud finds its active expression in the surrealist movement which followed him and first manifests itself as dadaism, a cultivation of meaninglessness and contradiction for its own sake. The surrealist message was that violence was the only adequate method of expression. At the same time that it exalted crime and violence, it proclaimed man's innocence and anti-theism. Although in its pessimism the surrealist movement has found an affinity with revolutionary communism, still it is neither a religion nor a politics; it is an "impossible wisdom."

Surrealism, if it has not changed the world, has furnished it with some strange myths which in part justify Nietzsche when he announced the return of the Greeks. In part only, for it is a question of the Greece of the shades, that of mysteries and black gods. Finally, even as Nietzsche's experiment is crowned in the acceptance of the noon, that of surrealism culminates in the exaltation of midnight, the obstinate anguished worship of the storm.[8]

In this survey of metaphysical revolt it was the intention of Albert Camus to show that the protest, defiance, and destruction that characterize man's rebellion against God is, in fact, the result of man's desire for a truer life. If, in some instances, this revolt has terminated in destruction and murder, it is nonetheless true that man in revolt has been driven by his need for order and morality. "Their conclusions have been disastrous or liberticidal only after they have rejected the burden of revolt, fled the tension that it imposes, and chosen the comfort of tyranny or slavery."[9] In every case revolt has been a protest against that in the universe which is dissonant, opaque, or a proposed solution for the continuity of life. In every case there has been a demand for unity. If the rebel protests against death, it is because he desires a meaningful life and cannot see how there can be meaning in a world where nothing is justified because nothing lasts. The rebel seeks an explanation for his happiness as well as his pain. The rebel, "without knowing it, is searching for an ethic or a holiness. Revolt is an ascetic discipline [*ascèse*], although groping. If the rebel blasphemes, then, it is in the hope for a new God."[10] Camus avows what should have been evident from the beginning of this study of his thought, i.e., the essentially religious quality of his philosophical concerns. The term, *ascèse*, is a rarely used French word designating the science of asceticism; from this point onward we constantly find it in Camus' description of revolt. Camus is a "rebel" and rests squarely in the tradition of what he calls "*la pensée révoltée*." He has learned much from the philosophical rebels, especially from Dostoievski and Nietzsche, but he, more consciously than either of these men, is attempting to regain that stability of outlook and creative relation with the world that was the fruit of the Christian world-view. The use of the expression "metaphysical revolt" to characterize the dominant philosophical temper of the modern world is an effort of clarification. The revolt has been a religious protest, contesting the accepted ultimate ends of human existence, traditionally held by the occidental Christian world. From the Christian point of view this revolt is simply a mad destruction of all order and meaning in the universe, proposed by irrational or demented philosophers. Camus' position, which counters the Christian view-point, is that the expanded understanding which critical reason has brought to the world, destroys the foundations of the Christian world-view and leaves thoughtful men compromised between a false unity and a true disunity. The rebel thinkers are those who have brought this contradiction to an acute point and chosen the alternative of a dimly conceived truth, the vague perception of unity that Camus feels is the affirmative heart of the experience of revolt. The value of his study of the metaphysical revolt is that Camus employs an interpretive guide which brings meaning to the strangeness of this philosophy and enables him to criticize the various conclusions of these thinkers who have sought to articulate this dimly perceived truth. The "even if" of Ivan Karamazov and Nietzsche's appeal for "new laws" are the high points of the developing clarity of this search for unity. The nihilism reached by other rebels is the result of their abandonment of the original demands of their revolt. But we learn, as well, from these aberrations.

Each time that it [revolt] deifies the total refusal of what is, the absolute no, it kills. Each time that it blindly accepts what is, and proclaims the absolute yes, it kills. Hatred of the Creator can turn into hatred of the creation or into an exclusive and alluring love of what is. But in both cases, it ends in murder and loses the right to be called revolt.[11]

That the nihilistic aberration of revolt leads to murder is what Camus seeks to prove in his study of the revolutionary efforts of the last two centuries. When the movement of revolt is translated into revolutionary action there are moments of triumph when the revolt is held to in faith, but the greater part of revolutionary action has ended in homicide or else regicide and deicide, betraying the one value of revolt and inaugurating the epoch of nihilism in which we now live.

HISTORICAL REVOLT

Regicides and Deicides

The year 1789 marks the time when the *idea* of a king was first killed. Under the "divine right" principle grace was put above justice as the prerogative of the king. But once God had been denied by a philosophy of revolt the king's prerogative of grace was meaningless; only justice could be tolerated by a people in revolt. There was no possibility of a compromise between the realms of grace and justice, and the king stood on the side of grace, claiming the support of a bogus God. Thus, the revolution was prepared. The ideological foundations of this revolution were laid by Rousseau who, in his *Social Contract* sets up reason as God and sees the public will to be God's representative on earth. For Rousseau, the body politic takes on the former attributes of God; the natural freedom and reason which characterize all men means that the general will is the expression of universal reason. Everything must submit to this will; that which does not may be justly destroyed. These were the foundations of the French Revolution and the dawn of a new religion, which began, observes Camus, by destroying the scaffolds of the king-priest only to rebuild them later as the altar of a new dogmatic religion.

Louis XVI was killed because he was God's earthly representative. According to revolutionary philosophy, his crime was theological, i.e., by the pretention of his very existence he has sinned against the divinity of the people. There are no

94

possible grounds for forgiveness; he must cease to exist. "Certainly, it is a repugnant scandal to have presented the public execution of a weak and good man as a great moment in our history. This scaffold does not mark a summit, it falls short of it."[12] The Revolution thinks to have freed man from God by destroying his historic representative. But if one God was lost, another was gained: reason, which is nothing but the "old god, disincarnated, cleanly detached from any relation with the earth and, like a balloon, sent back again into the empty sky of great principles."[13]

The Revolution opens into an era of formal morality, whose principles are set forth in the thought of Saint-Just. Morality is a political phenomenon: the expression of the will of the people. It follows that if there is crime it is due to moral weakness. But there should be no crime; the morality of the law which proceeds from the people should result in perfect unity. If factionalism should appear to mar this unity, then for the sake of this unity the non-conformists must be punished by the law. Thus, in the thought of Saint-Just, the Terror is totally justified. A religion of virtue comes to be founded on the law; if the people become discontent, then they are at fault, not the law, for the law is innocent. The French Revolution had gone full circle when the people found themselves once again under the oppression of the absolute. As the revolutionary passion cooled, the original conformity broke down and factionalism became an increasing political problem. In terms of the Roman legal system of Saint-Just, the dissenters should be destroyed, but soon there were too many of them. The result was that the people were compromised by the law and the law compromised by the people. The principles of the new religion failed, and Saint-Just went to his death without understanding why the people would not conform to Reason.

The transformation by which the Revolution replaced king and God by law and the people had stability only so long as the people did not come into conflict with the law. But this conflict came, and, from that moment on, the law had no justification except in a principle which had sprung from a people in revolt, had become absolutized and then found itself opposed by the people. This is a demonstration of Camus' observation that revolutions cannot be definitive, because the clear and abstract idea with which they begin does not adjust as the people themselves change. The revolutionary principle is predestined to conflict with the shifting ground from which it sprang. But if the regime persists in forcing this principle onto the people, there is a reversion to nihilism in which there are but the two alternatives of individual terrorism on one hand or state terrorism on the other. Both of these alternatives are characteristic of the political life of the 20th century.

Despite the regicide brought about by the theorists of the French Revolution, the true objective of deicide never came to pass. The final severance of God from the earth was to be the contribution of Hegel, whom Camus terms the "Napoleonic philosopher." The transcendental principles of justice, reason, and truth, consecrated by the French revolution, are embodied by Hegel into the flow of events of the concrete universal. But, in the course of this transmutation into the dynamics of becoming, these principles serve no longer as points of departure in thought and action; rather, they are goals. This means that if one begins in truth, he is not, *ipso facto*, assured of realizing final truth; in fact, such a beginning may impede this realization. With these principles now relegated to the end of history there is nothing remaining to guide us in reaching them except action itself. It is Camus' thesis that with the philosophy of Hegel and its subsequent development in 19th century German thought the history of revolt is profoundly transformed. In terms of this philosophy human nature is not yet realized, and man is called to action in order to bring about this final realization. The only rule of action, seen by Camus in Hegelian thought, is action itself. With Hegel begins the philosophy of efficacity whose consequences are to be seen in the rational and irrational state terrorism of the 20th century.

In the *Phenomenology of Mind* Camus finds the essential outlines of this philosophy of efficacity. According to Hegel, man is an animal who finds self-consciousness only through his desire for something beyond himself, which means principally to be recognized as oneself by other consciousnesses. This desire for recognition is the struggle of life, and history itself will be complete at the time when all men are recognized by all other men. But in the course of the struggle itself mankind is divided into those whose selfhood is recognized by others and those who are not, i.e., masters and slaves. It is only in this sort of societal division that the world process moves: the master serves to lead the slaves into action and creation in which the slaves increasingly free themselves from the bondage of nature. Human liberty can only be conquered through the slaves' transformation of the natural world into a technical world. The slaves themselves desire freedom from their condition and at the same time desire freedom from their master. This is the tension of the world process in which the master is bound to his role of master lest he be destroyed, and in which the slave is bound to his role as slave unless he revolt and become master himself. History, then, is the history of work and revolt.

Hegelian philosophy has delivered us from transcendence and has laid the groundwork for a marriage of metaphysical revolt with the revolutionary movement. Camus understands that all value judgment has been abandoned; the only moral axiom is conformity to the life and customs of one's nation, provided they survive against revolutionary attack. Hence, we are led immediately into the political cynicism of a world caught between the bare forces of masters and slaves, a world without principles and without innocence. This philosophy engendered a type of nihilism in which men are anxious to die, so that their sacrifice would bring them an aristocratic quality in regard to the final truth which is about to break. Violence and destruction become the first steps toward creation.

In its later interpretation and application, Hegel's thought was without difficulty purged of its mysticism and its God by men like Strauss, Bauer, and Feuerbach. Atheistic materialism automatically links with political revolution, since the negation of God's power means that man will take over his functions. The revolutionaries of the next century were to make full use of the Hegelian system for the final discrediting of the formal virtues of bourgeois life. The revolutionary thought which sprang from Hegel's system is fundamentally nihilistic. It has no path to follow but that of action and the truth or error of such action will not be determined until the end of history. In the arbitrariness of such a world one can do anything or do nothing: both alternatives are nihilistic.

The cynicism, the deification of history and matter, individual terror or state criminality, these inordinate consequences will then be born, fully armed, from an equivocal conception of the world which grants to history alone the function of producing values and truth.[14]

In a world devoid of God and value, total inaction or total destruction amount to the same thing in principle. The deicide has come to pass and man, freed from the bondage of God, is yet to achieve his freedom in nihilism and efficacity.

The divinity of man is still on the march and its worship will come only at the end of time. This apocalypse must be served and, lacking a God, at least a church must be built. . . . The sky is empty and the earth given up to a power without principles. Those who have chosen to kill and those who have chosen to be slaves will successively occupy the front of the stage, in the name of a revolt turned away from its truth.[15]

The Fastidious Murderers and the
Play, Les Justes

The translation of revolt into revolutionary action has, in the estimate of Albert Camus, largely resulted in a betrayal of

the original values of the revolt by a legitimatization of terror
and murder. What the French Revolution began, and what
radical Hegelianism perfected, finds its historic culmination in
fascism and Marxist-Stalinism. The history of these revolutions
is interpreted by Camus to be man's progressive deification of
himself. As will be discussed presently, this tendency combines
with the radical Hegelian philosophy to "give to Caesar those
functions which formerly belonged to God."

In the midst of this general movement of revolutionary
nihilism, Camus points out that a handful of young Russian
terrorists constitute the unique example of fidelity to the
values of revolt. These were the *"meurtriers délicats"* of 1905.

From the 1820's onward, young Russians, under the impact
of German and particularly Hegelian philosophy, became the
passionate incarnations of this philosophy. They accepted a
life without transcendence and became revolutionaries or, after
1878, terrorists. The various forms of nihilism which resulted
are seen in men like Belinsky or Pisarev, Bakunin, and Net-
chaiev, the latter three whom Camus calls the "possessed."[16]
With the assassination of General Trepov in 1878 there begins
what seems to be a general period of individual terrorism over
most of the world. In terrorism, nihilistic thought became
action, and in most cases claimed no value for justification.
The young terrorists of 1905 were an exception to this; they
were sustained by their common revolt against the oppression
which weighed upon their countrymen.

Above their executioners and themselves they placed the supreme and painful value that we have already found at the origins
of revolt. Let us at least pause to examine this value in the moment
when, for the last time in our history, the spirit of revolt meets the
spirit of compassion.[17]

The importance of this group of terrorists for the thought of
Albert Camus becomes apparent when we learn that *Les
Justes*, a play, was written by Camus in 1949 dramatizing what
he feels to be the capital moment in the career of Ivan Kalia-

yev and the group of "fastidious murders."[18] This play is an imaginative reconstruction of a particular period in the life of this group, and Camus employs as often as possible statements attributed to one or another person of the group. The incident concerns the assassination of the Grand Duke Serge by the young Kaliayev who threw a bomb into his carriage. During the first attempted assassination Kaliayev awaited the carriage of the Grand Duke, but did not throw the bomb because two children were with him. His comrades approved him in this. The Grand Duke was alone during the following attempt, and the assassination was successful. Kaliayev was arrested and later hanged.

The remarkable feature of this group and especially Kaliayev is that theirs is not simply a revolutionary fanaticism motivated by hatred for the oppressive monarchy and blind love for the idea of revolution. Kaliayev, who is nick-named "the Poet," finds his reason for revolt neither in hatred nor abstract principles but in love for living. When some find him a little unusual for a terrorist he says,

I would like to explain to them that I am not extraordinary. They find me a little crazy, too impulsive. But, evenso, like them I believe in the idea. Like them I want to sacrifice myself. I too, I can be clever, taciturn, secretive, efficacious. Only, life goes on seeming marvellous to me. I love beauty, happiness! This is why I hate despotism. How can this be explained to them? The revolution, certainly! But revolution for life, to give a chance to life, do you understand?[19]

But Kaliayev must kill another man in order to fight against despotism; he knows as well that he too will die because of the murder. To kill another man for an idea is one thing, but, for Kaliayev, to die oneself for that idea is a categorically different act, an act which somehow justifies him, e.g.,

Do you understand why I asked to throw the bomb? To die for the idea, this is the only way to be at the height of the idea. It is the justification. . . . One thought torments me: They have made assassins out of us. But at the same time I think that I am going to die and my heart becomes calm. I smile, you see, and I go back to sleep like an infant.[20]

Alongside the ideas which are properly that of *la pensée révoltée*, Camus has vividly contrasted the more familiar thought of the hardened revolutionary in the person of Stepan. After the first attempt when Kaliayev refused to throw the bomb because of the children, Stepan meets this news with disgust. This is nonsense, he says, "when we decide to forget about children, that will be the day when we shall be masters of the world." One of the group, Dora, says that humanity would hate them if the revolution proceeded on this basis. Stepan then replies that if one loves humanity enough he should not be hindered by its scruples; if humanity refuses to kill children in order to save itself and puts itself in the way of the revolution it will be struck down "if it is necessary and until it understands. I too, I love the people."[21] There are two types of terrorism, i.e., that which proceeds from revolt and that which proceeds from revolution. The clarity and necessity of the latter makes it imperative that the revolutionary idea be realized, because it is, by definition, good. The less certain quality of the former is due to its awareness of a limit imposed upon human action. This is the central message of *Les Justes* and is expressed by Dora, i.e.,

Yanek [Kaliayev] agrees to kill the Grand-Duke since his death can bring the time nearer when Russian children will no longer die of hunger. That in itself is not easy. But the death of the nephews of the Grand-Duke will not prevent any children from dying of hunger. Even in destruction there is an order, there are limits.[22]

A short while before Kaliayev goes out to assassinate the Grand Duke he confesses to Dora that he has come to realize how difficult it is to kill, that hatred is not a sufficient reason for such an act. He wants to push the motives for his revolutionary action to their extreme end and go beyond hatred. When Dora says that there is nothing beyond hatred, Kaliayev replies, "There is love."[23] Before going out, Kaliayev crosses himself before an icon.

After the assassination and arrest Kaliayev is in prison. He is visited by Skouratov, head of the police: a sly and sophisticated man whose confidence and cynicism lead him into a dialogue very much like those found in the works of Arthur Koestler in which the proponents of the new and old worlds face one another in a quiet, terrifying struggle. Skouratov holds out the hope of pardon to the prisoner, provided he repent of his crime publicly. But Kaliayev is not a criminal and has committed no crime; he has committed an act of justice and is ready to die for it. He corrects Skouratov by saying, "I am a prisoner of war, not an accused."[24] Later, he is visited by the Grand Duchess who, slightly deranged following her husband's death, fervently pleads with Kaliayev to repent and embrace the Christian faith. But, even though faced intimately with a woman who has been torn by his action, Kaliayev never loses a lucid conception of the nature of his revolt. As for the Church, he says, it has changed somewhat; "it has kept the grace for itself and has left us the duty of exercising charity."[25] The Grand Duchess tells him that there is no love apart from God, and Kaliayev replies "Yes. Love for the creature."[26]

After the trial and Kaliayev's sentence of execution, the little group of terrorists are together attempting to understand and absorb what has taken place. It is the night when Kaliayev is to be executed, and they await the news of this. They repeat some of the statements which he had made during his trial, e.g., "Death will be my supreme protest against a world of tears and blood. . . . If I be at the height of the human protest against violence, may death crown my work with the purity of the idea."[27] The fastidious murderers realize the painful contradiction in which they are living. They have given themselves to the terrorist protest against the misery which is the lot of the Russian people, but they know that the protest of this revolt is governed by limits residing in the positive value which they seek. Kaliayev has taught them that the hatred of the "no" is secondary to the love of human beauty and happiness which is the "yes," activating the protest. They understand that revolt is a tension without resolution which cannot end in comfort or dogmatism without losing its value. But Dora expresses the fear that other revolutionaries might not understand the limits which they recognized, e.g., "Perhaps others will come who will authorize themselves to kill in our name and who will not pay with their life."[28]

In a letter written in 1950 and published in the revue, *Caliban*, Albert Camus outlines the response which the 1905 rebels would make to the problem whether a rebel could kill a prison guard, knowing that he had children. Their response would be, the following:

1) There are limits. Children are a limit (there are yet others);
2) In an extraordinary circumstance one can kill the guard, in the name of justice;
3) But one must himself accept to die.[29]

Camus' own estimate of the significance of the life of Kaliayev and his comrades is seen in *L'Homme révolté*, i.e.,

Such a great forgetfulness of self, allied with such a profound care for the lives of others, permits us to suppose that these fastidious murderers lived the destiny of revolt in its most extreme contradiction. One may believe that they also, held that it was unjustified. Necessary and inexcusable, it is thus that murder appeared to them. Mediocre hearts, confronted with this terrible problem, can find peace in forgetting one of the terms. They will be content, in the name of formal principles, to find all immediate violence inexcusable and will thus permit this general violence on the scale of the world and history. Or, in the name of history, they will persuade themselves that violence is necessary, and will thus add murder to murder, to the point that history is but a long violation of all that in man protests against injustice. This defines the two faces of contemporary nihilism; bourgeois and revolutionary.[30]

Kaliayev and his fellow terrorists lived in this contradiction and triumphed over nihilism, but this triumph was to be unique and short-lived. Presently, the revolutionaries in Russia move in paths of political cynicism, and, from this point onward, sterility sets in.

IRRATIONAL TERROR

The spirit of revolt gave birth to many revolutions in the 20th century. According to Camus, all of these revolutions led either to a rational or to an irrational glorification of the state and in both cases issued into a state terrorism. The regimes under Hitler and Mussolini were examples of irrational states, whose strength proceeded from the supposition that history is the meaningless product of aimless force. "Fascism," says Camus, "is contempt."[31] The fascist regimes of Germany and Italy found their definition and force in that which they scorned. The movement of such a state is dependent upon its enemies, and once this primary direction is given the fascist regime thrives on a pure dynamism of perpetual movement and negation. In the Hitlerian revolution the goal of this dynamism was a vague anti-Christian empire of the soldier-workers, not unlike the ultimate Marxist dream. In the Hitlerian regime modern statism finds its true form and its ultimate perversion of revolt, i.e., it becomes a religion. To be part of the Nazi state one participated in a religion whose God was the *Führer* and whose faith was National-Socialism, both of which commanded absolute obedience. In such a state only the *Führer* assumed responsibility and the consequent innocence or guilt of the state. But, by definition, the state was innocent, and those against whom the state set itself were, by definition, guilty. This conception made possible the desperate slaughter of those who might otherwise have been considered innocent; the guilty, the enemy, the dead, all of these were equivalent in the outward movement of the irrational and frenetic pride of a nation.

Camus' brief analysis of the principles which motivated the "irrational terror" of fascism is more obvious and considerably less interesting than the longer study of "rational terror." The conclusion of the essay is that Nazism was never more than a provincially oriented primitive urge which had no basis for stability or for its fervent claim to be eternal and universal. Camus feels that Nazism is to be judged not only by its murders but also for its willed destruction of Germany in the mad presumption that if Germany was not victorious it had no right to live. The desperate expansion of the fascist state, if it was unsuccessful, meant not surrender but suicide.

Written during and partly after the Occupation, Camus' *Lettres à un ami allemand* reveal the admirable breadth of spirit that makes all of his political writings remarkable. These four letters, addressed to an anonymous German friend of pre-war days, were carefully weighed attempts to formulate a hopeful and just attitude for the people of France in expectation of the defeat of the Nazi regime. This was a difficult task to achieve, given the bitterness of France's defeat and its liberation primarily by forces not its own. Camus sought to steer between the natural temptations of hatred, on one hand, and *je-m'en-fichisme* on the other.

From a point of philosophical interest the fourth letter is the most important. Here we see, actually for the first time, the budding concept of "revolt" as it was later to be developed. The interest lies in the fact that Camus and his German friend take the same level of discussion: neither believes that the world has any higher meaning. From this point on, the German feels justified in giving himself to the Nazi dream of conquest. But this is not the only alternative for one who has been delivered from transcendence. Camus marks out the other alternative in the following passage, i.e.,

To the contrary, I chose justice in order to remain faithful to the earth. I continue to believe that this world has no higher meaning. But I know that something in it does have meaning, and this is man, because he is the one being that demands it. This world at least possesses the truth of man, and our job is to find grounds for his justification against destiny itself. And there are no other grounds than man himself, and it is he that must be saved if one wants to save the idea which one has about life. Your smile and your disdain seem to say, "What is it to save man?" But I cry out to you with all my being that it is not to mutilate him, and it is to give him his chance for the justice of which he alone is able to conceive.[32]

Camus, as a Frenchman, is able to distinguish himself from the Nazi on the basis of the limits which he deems part of human nature itself. That there is a human nature is the thesis which Camus later has developed in his philosophy of revolt. Here, speaking for other French humanists, he puts forth a thoroughgoing humanism, e.g., "Our strength is to reflect, as you do, on the depth of the world, to refuse nothing in the drama which is our own, but, at the same time, at the end of this disaster of the intellect, to have saved the idea of man and to draw from it the indefatigable courage of renaissances."[33] Having taken this position, he, no more than his friend, is able to say what truth is, "but at least we know what falsehood is: this precisely is what you have taught us."[34] As will become more obvious in Chapter VII, the moral and political philosophy of Albert Camus emerges from his involvement in the suffering and death of the historical upheaval of the mid-20th century. And the discovery of "limits" as a guide to human thought and action owes no small part to his countrymen's struggle with the "irrational terror" which reigned over their land.[35]

RATIONAL TERROR

The long analytical and critical essay which Albert Camus has devoted to Marxist thought and its historical impact constitutes the most ambitious historical-ideological criticism in *L'Homme révolté*. It has been this section that has gained wide acclaim for Camus both in France and abroad; and it is also this section which has merited bitter attacks, primarily from Marxist philosophers and Communist party journals. Camus has here developed some of the central critical theses of *L'Homme révolté* in regard to the perversion which he finds wrought to the values of revolt. The general thesis of the critical essays of *L'Homme révolté* is that modern revolutions, springing out of the modern metaphysical revolt, have been the progressive deification of man; that these revolutions have issued into nihilism and terror because of their placing of value completely above history (e.g., the French Revolution) or of identifying value absolutely with history (e.g., the fascist and Soviet states). Under this general thesis, the critique of post-Hegelian nihilism is of signal importance, and three additional critical theses make their appearance in this essay on Marxist theory and practice, to wit: (1) the criticism of prophetic Marxism, (2) the criticism of the dialectical contradictions of the idea of the end of history, and (3) the criticism of the notion of objective guilt. We shall examine these theses in this same order.

Camus makes a sharp distinction between Marxist social criticism and Marxist Utopianism. He recognizes the value of the former and its permanent contribution to social study.[36] But it is Marxist Utopianism with which he is concerned because it was this prophetic dream that was followed by the builders of the Russian communist state and not the critical method.

Prophetic Marxism, in the estimation of Albert Camus, is indebted to both the Christian faith and bourgeois culture for its content. In contrast to the Greek cyclical view of history, both prophetic Marxism and Christianity share a developmental idea of history's moving toward an apocalypse. Both Christians and Marxists reject the world as it is, superimpose a symbolical or ideological structure over it by way of transformation, and then await its end.

These symbols are those of the divine drama which unfolds itself through time. Nature is no longer but the setting for this drama. The beautiful equilibrium of man and nature, the consent of man to the world, which brings to the light and makes for the brilliance of all ancient thought, this was broken to the profit of history, first of all by Christianity.[37]

Camus cites Joseph de Maistre as an example of the common world-view held by Marxism and the Christian faith. Both are political realists and both seek to establish a new order.

Marxism shares the common attitude of bourgeois culture in its cult of progress, of technique and industry, and the belief that science can aid man to conquer nature. But this optimism in progress, says Camus, is founded on a condition which justifies such an attitude, thus revealing in both attitudes a conservatism. Marx has borrowed heavily from the bourgeois economists, Compte and Ricardo, to construct, like them, an economic system for a steam engine-textile world—not for an electrical-atomic age.

The revolutionary quality of the Marxist prophecy was the argument that history was not only dialectically, but was economically determined. There are no transcendental principles, and the economic substructure of history reveals that the "virtues" cherished by the bourgeoisie are, in reality, founded on human misery and labor. It is Marx's true greatness, for Camus, that the dignity of labor is his central ethic. But the revolution which is to vindicate this ethic is to be realized without any transcendent or ethical basis for a working justice and dignity. It is history which will bring about this revolution, made possible by the high productivity created in the capitalist economy. Capitalism moves inevitably toward this final revolution, which is final because it is the triumph of the universal over the particular, in short, the end of history.

We see, then, that after having negated God and all transcendent principles, Marx replaces this with the "future." The future is the sole value, hope, and justification for this present life, and, consequently anything which serves this future is *ipso facto,* a value. The absolute identification of value with a future Utopia leads easily into opportunism and ruthlessness; prophetic Marxism prepares the destruction of all human revolt in the name of a distant Golden Age. Thus, "scientific socialism" ceased to be scientific the moment it turned from social analysis to an absolute prophecy of the future.

The non-scientific nature of prophetic Marxism is precisely the reason why the Utopia has not come to pass. The radical polarity between capital and labor was not realized for the reason that history is not solely determined by economic factors. The influence of labor unions, national conflicts, the technological division of the proletariat, these not unfamiliar factors are put forth by Camus as new conditions which undermine the Marxist prophecy. In effect the proletariat has rejected the historic task which Marx gave it. And in the Russian economy itself the bourgeois practice of reinvesting profits is being followed in the worship of productivity, leaving the proletariat much in the same condition it has always been, awaiting a distant future. Rather than ameliorating the degrading aspects of labor, the communist state has sought to glorify them in the name of productivity. Hence, prophetic Marxism is found to be in contradiction with science as well as economics and is a faith which is no more founded on pure reason than other prophetic faiths. Camus compares this long wait for the Utopia to that of the early Christians awaiting the end of the world; when the end did not come, an adjustment had to be made to an ongoing existence. In order to justify themselves, the Marxists, like the Church, must ignore and deny new historical and economic truths.

The contradictions within the idea of the end of history are manifest in Lenin's *State and Revolution.* Here, Lenin roundly condemns the character of the bourgeois state and its use of police force for the repression of the already economically oppressed proletariat. Lenin states that the coming to power of the proletariat will mean the end of oppression by police. But later, Camus points out, Lenin admits that, during the dictatorship of the proletariat, police action will be necessary to repress exploiters who seek to subvert the workers' revolution. Lenin goes on to say that this period of police vigilance will have an indefinite length and an unforeseeable time limit before the appearance of the final communist society. And thus it has been, remarks Camus, for the past thirty years since the Russian Revolution: an eternal crusade, an imperialism of justice, using injustice, lies, and crime in order to arrive at the sudden mystical transformation which will bring liberty and justice.

In strict fidelity to the dialectical concept of history, can the Marxist actually substantiate the doctrine of the end of history? For the Christian, history has an end because it has a beginning. But for the Marxist there never was such a beginning, and Camus argues that a complete acceptance of the dialectical postulate would mean that the final synthesis would never take place.

But if one admits the dialectical postulate, it must be entirely admitted. Even as the society with orders gave way to a society without orders but with classes, one must recognize that the society of classes will give way to a society without classes but animated by a new antagonism yet to be defined. A movement, to which a beginning is refused, cannot have an end. "If socialism," says a libertarian essayist, "is an eternal becoming, its means are its ends." Exactly so, it has no end; there are only the means which are guaranteed by nothing, unless it be by a value which is foreign to becoming. In this sense it is correct to remark that the dialectic is not and cannot be revolutionary. According to our point of view, it is only nihilistic, pure movement which seeks to negate all that is not itself.[38]

Camus finds no justification for the Marxist doctrine of the end of history. But the insistence of Marxists on this unjustified principle comes to a positing of a dogma, an article of faith which serves neither as a value nor a rule of conduct but simply as a principle of terror. Revolutionary Marxism, which claims itself to be "scientific," can now be quietly denounced as a faith. Marxism, which had seen its task as the great representative of human justice against a world of grace, has, in its own movement, lost its rebellious spirit and begun a struggle with truth itself. Having sprung from the noble aspirations of revolt, the great Revolution has absolutized all value at the end of becoming and now moves in an "eternal becoming," destroying revolt, justice, and truth. In a striking manner, Camus summarizes this movement, i.e.,

How can one live without grace? This is the question which dominated the 19th century. "By justice," replied those who did not wish to accept absolute nihilism. To the peoples who were losing faith in the kingdom of heaven, they promised the kingdom of man. The preaching of the city of man grew more frequent until the end of the 19th century when it became visionary and put the certitudes of science to the service of the Utopia. But the kingdom has become further removed, prodigious wars have ravaged the most ancient of lands, the blood of rebels has covered the walls of towns, and total justice has come no nearer. The question of the 20th century, for which the 1905 terrorists died and which tears the contemporary world, has little by little become clear: how can one live without grace and without justice?

To this question only nihilism, and not revolt, has replied. Up to this time it alone has spoken, taking up once more the formula of the romantic rebels: "Frenzy." Historical frenzy is called power.[39]

With final justice as its alleged goal the communist state follows its will to power by the armed conquest of nations and continents. The metaphysical revolt has lost its true principles and moves forward in its "obstinate scholasticism."

The third critical thesis employed by Camus in his study of the Marxist state is that the communist state operates with the presumption of the objective guilt of its people. Under the perverted dogmatism of the communist state, liberty can only be understood as total enslavement. This is because, being free from God, man must absolutely submit himself to the coming of the final Kingdom which involves expansion, war, and tyranny. This absolute submission is the price that must be paid for the Kingdom and will be necessary for an indefinite period. But, Camus remarks, while this period lasts there is equally an indefinite negation of the end which is the sole justification for enslavement.

While awaiting the moment of its complete world domination the communist empire achieves temporal domination within its own orbit by the negation of history and its reformulation in accord with the patterns prescribed by the Marxist laws of change and development. Nothing escapes this constant negation and revision. Camus explains this practice as the result of the supposition of *the infinite plasticity of men*, which is to say that there is no human nature. He contends that the negation of human nature is a basic tenet in the functioning of Russian Marxism. Men must be conceived as "things" so that they can be accorded with the larger system of the state. This is why the Freudian claim of the existence of an irrational, subconscious realm in man is utterly denied. The Russian state can only recognize the social ego of men, and thus conceives mankind as a play of forces that can be rationally directed and molded. Given the infinite plasticity of men there is nothing improper in the negation of history and its recreation. There is no human basis for objecting to this. Even those who are condemned by the state are made to serve the system by confessing their evil and admitting that their death is justified. All things are rationally transformed into accord with the system. This is why it is termed the "rational terror."

It is here that Camus' critique of the Marxist state has become most trenchant, because it is here that the basis of his philosophy of revolt (that there is a human nature) is most directly challenged. Consequently, the Marxist state is seen as a fundamental contradiction to the spirit of revolt which was its original impetus. The *verdinglichung* of men, which was at the heart of Marx's protest, has now become a ruling principle in his name. This presumption of man's infinite plasticity underlies the practice of "brain-washing."

From this point of view the only psychological revolution that our times have known since Freud has been accomplished by the N.K.V.D. and the political police in general. Guided by a deterministic hypothesis, calculating the weak points and the degree of elasticity of souls, these new techniques have pushed back the limits of man still more and attempt to prove that no individual psychology is original, and that the common measure of character is the thing. They have literally created a physics of souls.[40]

From this point on, human relations are transformed. Friendship is no longer possible except through the state to which absolute allegiance is required. Dialogue between men has been replaced by propaganda and polemics, which is only a type of monologue. Russian Marxism has become an earthly religion which affirms the absolute innocence of history and the guilt of men. Any delay in the coming of the Utopia is not the fault of the historic pattern but is due to the sin of man. Failure means guilt and merits immediate punishment. Inversely, whoever succeeds is declared heroic in the name of history. These are the necessary consequences of a regime where efficacity and means are the sole existent values. Beginning with an affirmation of human innocence, revolt has now become the rational terror which affirms the general guilt of men, and has faith that the end of history will justify this affirmation—if it comes.

The critical study which Albert Camus has made of revolt in history has attempted to show that, in usurping God's functions, the rational and irrational empires have ended in terror and slavery and have created submen rather than supermen. Whether the hangman exalts himself, as in Nazism, or is exalted by his victims, as in the communist state, in either case the motivating spirit is no longer revolt but consent. Revolution has betrayed its origins by seeking the shortest way to earthly immortality, i.e., nihilism and terror. This is the spirit in which most of Europe lives today, but Camus is offering no justification for that part of society which is not, as yet, struck by the revolution. On many occasions Camus has remarked that bourgeois society has no grounds for condemning the perversions of the revolutions, inasmuch as it is the injustice of that society which lies at the root of this revolution. The condemnation of the revolutionary states does not mean that we can now repose in self-satisfaction, for this would be an acceptance and sanctification of man's plight. The revolution has begun contradicting itself, and it is for others to seize these values which the revolution still preaches and to realize them. The contradiction of the revolution, as revealed in Camus' critique, is that it is no longer in revolt. And when the revolutionary is no longer in revolt he is a functionary. Revolt is the refusal of being reduced to history, it is the refusal of being treated as a "thing." At the same time it is an affirmation of a nature which is common to all men and beyond the reach of history or its power. Moreover, it is not totality which revolt demands, but unity. When revolution attempts to force a total unanimity it negates human nature and pits itself against revolt. Man has not revolted against God, only to give God's power to Caesar. But this is precisely the perversion that revolution has brought about. Consequently, the paramount struggle today is between caesarism and revolt. For its part, revolt can offer no formal ethic; it can serve only as a guide which, in action, gradually reveals more and more of the value which was originally invoked.

Returning once more to the figure of Prometheus, the first of mankind's many rebels, Camus has written this short parable which is a cogent résumé for the whole chapter on revolt and history, i.e.,

Here, the surprising itinerary of Prometheus is completed. Shouting his hatred of the gods and his love for man, he turns away from

Zeus in contempt and comes to the mortals to lead them in an assault on heaven. But men are weak, or cowardly; they must be organized. They love pleasure and immediate happiness; they must be taught to refuse their daily honey in order to grow. Thus, Prometheus, in his turn, becomes a master who teaches at first, later commands. The battle still goes on and becomes exhausting. Men doubt that they will reach the city of the sun and even that it exists. They must be saved from themselves. The hero then tells them that he knows the city and he is the sole person to know it. Those who doubt this will be thrown into the desert, nailed to a rock, and offered up to the vicious birds. Henceforth, the others will walk in the shadows, behind the pensive and lonely master. Prometheus, solitary, has become God and reigns over the solitude of men. But from Zeus he has conquered nothing but solitude and cruelty; he is no longer Prometheus, he is Caesar. The true, the eternal Prometheus, now has the face of one of his victims. The same cry, come from the depth of the ages, sounds forever at the bottom of the Scythian desert.[41]

CHAPTER VII

THE POLITICAL

PHILOSOPHY OF REVOLT

IN THE spring of 1953 Albert Camus delivered an address before the Bourse de Travail of Saint-Etienne,[1] in the course of which he made the observation that the protagonists and guardians of freedom have always been the oppressed. The towns and bourgs of the Middle Ages, under pressure of the feudal society, became centers of ferment for liberty, whose demand was to find a fleeting triumph during the French Revolution. The inheritors of this tradition in the 19th century were the laboring groups, who, under the oppression which they experienced in a bourgeois society, became the defenders not only of freedom, but also of justice. The tragedy of the Marxist movement has been that, in condemning this bourgeois conception of freedom, they condemned all freedom, relegating it to the end of time, and became uniquely concerned with the attainment of justice. "And the dynamic intellectuals announced to the worker that it was bread alone that interested him and not freedom, as if the worker did not know that his bread depends as well on his freedom."[2] Faced with the conflicting values of freedom and justice, the revolutionary movement chose the latter. It was through this choice that the world's most hopeful revolution in 1917 was soon transformed into the world's most efficacious dictatorship, sustaining its power through state police. The result has been that our world today is divided by the cynical opposition of a society of injustice to a society of enslavement. But, in either case, the victim is the same, and it is his justice and his freedom that have been violated. The oppression goes on and the values proclaimed by man in revolt are yet to be recognized.

It is obvious that the idea of revolt developed by Camus lends itself to a positive political philosophy as well as to critical analysis. Although the concluding sections of *L'Homme révolté* set forth only a general political philosophy, Camus has elsewhere demonstrated that a philosophy of revolt can be completely engaged in the critical and creative task of political dialogue. It would be more correct to say that such a philosophy has existence only if it is engaged in this immediate task. The high-minded and thoughtful editorials, written by Camus while editor of the newspaper, *Combat*, are an admirable expression of the political relevance of Camus' philosophy of revolt.[3] Through these writings as well as through his letters, speeches, and interviews we discover a constructive political thought that shows Camus to be filling his role which is "seulement accepter le temps tel qu'il est, faire son metier en un mot."[4] In accepting the times such as they are, Camus cannot avoid addressing himself to the problems of fear and insecurity which afflict his epoch, nor keep from searching for a hopeful line of action which is consonant with the values that have been discovered in the revolt of modern man. The preoccupation with the problem and significance of death continues to dominate this aspect of his thought as it has appeared in all of his works from *Noces* onward. Even as the *raisonnement absurde* begins with the individual question of suicide, the philosophy of revolt begins with the social question of murder. The question, "Can one take his own life?" gives way to "Can one take the life of another?" In the first instance, the conclusion was that suicide was not the solution to the problem of life's absurdity. In the examination of revolt and history the conclusion was that the destruction of another person brings neither the solution to the problem posed by revolt nor the realization of its positive value of human solidarity. In order to understand better the guiding limit which underlies Camus' political thought let us make a closer examination of his thinking about the question of murder.

We have seen that after God was destroyed in the metaphysical revolt the revolutionary expression of revolt turned to the murder of men. But murder is an act which cannot be reconciled with revolt. This is because revolt affirms "we are," whereas the act of murder affirms that "we shall be" after other men have been destroyed. Murder cannot proceed from revolt, since it contradicts its value; if there be murder it can only be an exception to the rule which revolt makes clear.

The exception having taken place, the rule will again become possible. On the level of history, as in the individual life, murder is thus a desperate exception or it is nothing. The disruption that it causes in the order of things is without future. It is unwonted and thus can be neither used nor be systematic as the purely historical attitude would have it. It is the limit which one reaches only once, after which one must die. If he is brought to this point the rebel has only one way of reconciling himself to his murderous act: to accept his own sacrifice and death. He kills and dies so that it be clear that murder is impossible. He thus shows that in reality he prefers the *We are* to the *We shall be*.[5]

If, caught within an oppressive system, the rebel is driven to murder in the movement of protest, he must realize that this act is foreign to the reasons which motivate his protest; it is the exceptionable act which is forced upon him by the outward movement of his revolt. If he chooses that another should die, then he has no right to preserve his own life. He cannot justify his life as a murderer by the legitimacy of his revolt, because the value of revolt does not legitimatize murder. Hence, if he truly holds to this value which has been born within him, he will understand that this value can be vindicated only through his sacrifice. In placing this value above his own life he, like Kaliayev, discovers the "metaphysical honor" of men.

The outcome of revolt is not destruction, simply because it affirms something at the same time that it denies something else. It is this affirmation of the unity of all men in face of a common destiny that brings to light the evil of slavery, lying, and terror. The evil of these conditions is not posited on the basis of an abstract principle, but because they create silence and incommunicability between men and thus contradict the imperative value in the heart of the rebel. This is Camus' proposal of a value which is neither above history nor at its end, but is ever present in the ongoing history of men. For the rebel there can be no historical absolute; his one certainty is the not-too-certain consciousness of the limits which the value of revolt sets for him. This means that in all human ventures we can never be rid of risk. "If revolt was able to found a philosophy . . . this would be a philosophy of limits, of calculated ignorance and risk."[6] Unlike revolution, revolt can promise only a certain dignity and a relative justice.

The question, then, is whether such a philosophy can be efficacious in face of the abiding problems of political life. Camus believes that there are two central paradoxes in political affairs which have always created insoluble problems for those who seek ethical clarity in their political judgments. The first is the paradox which forces us to choose between violence and nonviolence. The second is the paradoxical choice between justice and freedom which plagues every revolution. The first of these antinomies presents itself as a choice between grace or history, God or the sword. But for a philosophy of limits the following position would be taken: nonviolence, as a policy, is necessarily limited by the fact that this policy may be consenting to the even greater violence of slavery. If this be the case, and if violence is necessary, then this can only be in the name of those institutions which we know will limit violence and not accept it as a rule. Such an institution would be that which shares the rebel's risk and uncertainty and therefore cannot freely take the lives of others to achieve its goal. In one of the finest paragraphs of *L'Homme révolté* Camus writes,

When the end is absolute, i.e., historically speaking, when one believes it to be certain, then one can go to the point of sacrificing others. When it is not, one can sacrifice only oneself in the battle for common dignity. Does the end justify the means? This is possible. But what will justify the end? To this question, which historical revolt leaves hanging, revolt replies: the means.[7]

Few passages in the writings of Albert Camus make so clear the moral insufficiency of absolute values and at the same time show so well that only a philosophy of limits can take a moral position which is faithful to the human condition.

Camus maintains that all revolutions have foundered on the antinomy of justice and freedom. To grant absolute freedom is to allow the strong to dominate the weak. To enforce absolute justice is to destroy freedom in a society. These two requirements which revolt sets forth become conflicts within revolutionary societies. But if our revolt is faithfully maintained, justice and freedom must exist together, each one limiting the other. A revolution, faithful to the human condition, will guarantee free expression immediately, not later; it will announce a code of civil rights now and not later. What injustice still exists must stand under open criticism in the future. The present then can bring us only a relative justice, but it brings also a "certain dignity" to the life of every man. Here again Camus takes a position which denies the relevance of transcendent values to the given conditions of human society. The critique of revolt in history has concluded that the attempt to realize immediate justice destroys freedom and *vice versa*; it has also concluded that political societies can never attain, e.g., absolute freedom or nonviolence by sublimating these values and relegating them to the end of an historical goal to be reached through injustice and violence. The historical critique of revolutions has, in Camus' estimation, amply demonstrated that there is no transcendental guarantee for human values or their achievement. Human values are active in the tensions of society or else they are not; to claim that they will exist in the future or do exist in heaven is tantamount to saying that they do not exist among men. A philosophy of limits is the answer made by Camus to the modern political tragedy of noble aspirations and tyrannical achievements.

The question has been posed as to the efficacity of a philosophy based on revolt. Camus now can reply

without hesitation that it is the only attitude today to be such. There are two kinds of efficacity, that of the typhoon and that of the sap. Historical absolutism is not efficacious, it is efficient; it has taken and held on to power. Once in possession of power it destroys the one creative reality. Intransigent and limited action, which is the expression of revolt, maintains this reality and attempts only to extend it more and more. It is not said that this line of action cannot conquer. It is said that it runs the risk of not conquering and dying. But revolution will either take this risk or else it will confess that it is nothing more than an undertaking of new masters, meriting the same contempt.[8]

The risk proposed by revolt is not a certain triumph, but after one hundred fifty years the revolutionaries themselves have had their optimism charred; their own failures should convince them that only in revolt will they again discover the origins which lay forgotten in the path of their frenzy.

We see, then, how Albert Camus' meditations on the significance of death have grown into a philosophical tool with incisive critical and creative edges. The solitary reflections of Sisyphus have given way to the efforts of Prometheus to formulate an earth-bound attitude which will do justice to the human condition. The concrete and *engagé* character of this attitude is due in large part, it appears, to the immediate pressures which came to bear on the thought of Camus during the course of his journalistic career. It is fair to say that the results of the *raisonnement absurde* never find expression in these editorials in *Combat*. The need to speak to a war-stricken nation apparently suppressed the thought of *The Myth of Sisyphus* even when it had just appeared in 1943. The early thought of Camus that finds a place in these writings is that of *Noces* and *L'Etranger* with its concern for death and the effects of moral legalism. This tends to confirm what we have already said at the conclusion of Part One, that the authentic thought of Albert Camus excludes the *raisonnement absurde* which is an aberration from the direction of thought laid out in *Noces* and *L'Etranger* and later rejoined in the conclusion of the play, *Caligula*.

The journalistic pieces accompany the emergence of France once more into national freedom; they are characterized by a quiet groping for an attitude which does justice to the past four years of occupation and yet leaves a positive hope for the future, an attitude which we have already seen in the *Lettres à un ami allemand*. In 1944, on the night of the liberation of Paris, he writes,

On the hottest and most beautiful of August nights the sky of Paris is a mixture of everpresent stars and of tracer bullets, of the smoke of conflagrations and the multicolored rockets of popular celebration. On this matchless night there comes to a close four years of a monstrous history and an indescribable struggle in which France was at grips with its shame and its fury.[9]

The intense solidarity, which all members of the *Résistance* felt, was shared in full by Camus. Within this solidarity Camus, like so many others, believed that there was hope for a political life deeply committed to the values of justice and freedom which had given substance to the *Résistance*. But toward the close of 1944 the conflicting parties of French political thought began to emerge, and the still-fresh feeling of solidarity begins to crumble. In an editorial of October 7, Camus makes the plea to the Communist party not to rush dogmatically ahead into polemics but to maintain the nation's solidarity in experimenting with an ethical-political program.[10] Throughout these editorials, of a period extending through 1947, there runs the concern to preserve the political unity of France, to create tolerance among the political parties and to accept this new beginning as the first chance which France has ever had to pursue a political life which is moderate, obstinate, and without illusions as to what will buttress the dignity of man. And during this three-year period Camus' journalistic pieces are already replete with the ideas which are later to be fused into a "philosophy of limits," e.g., the conflict of freedom and justice,[11] the need for constant political lucidity,[12] the necessity of using the right means in achieving just goals,[13] the critique of socialism's futuristic goals,[14] condemnation of violence as a continuing policy,[15] and the idea that the measure of a good political society is the passion and devotion of its individual members.[16]

In the Autumn of 1948 there appeared in *Combat* a series of articles under the general title, "Neither Victims nor Hangmen," which constitutes the first general statement of the developing philosophy of limits. We should remember that Camus was then in the midst of preparing the text of *L'Homme révolté*, which was, in all, a four year writing project. The first two editorials of this series are general critiques of the times; the following two are critiques of Marxist-socialism; the last four articles put forth positive proposals toward the possibility of achieving world peace and world order. It is important that this series of articles be examined in order to consolidate our understanding of Camus' philosophy as it has been outlined in his more formal works.

In the editorials, "The Century of Fear" and "Save the Bodies,"[17] Camus addresses himself to the political *malaise* of the 20th century, a century in which the technique of fear is being fully exploited. In general, Europeans are backed to the wall with the hopeless choice of condoning and engaging in killing in order to conquer and convince others of the rightness of their position, or else of being killed for the same reasons. Despite the repugnancy of this choice they do not protest, because they know that they cannot argue with blind forces and with intransigent abstractions. They know there can be no discussion with a man of ideology; this kind of man is incommunicable and therefore terrifying. Camus speaks here on the part of the oppressed, the "victims" of a Europe of battling ideologies and armies, both of which are murderous. What Camus sees to have happened is that dialogue between men has broken down; there is only the cacophony of many monologues, all attempting to realize their Utopias. The oppressed of Europe, who are victimized by this struggle, have the one alternative before them of reflecting on the nature of this fear which paralyzes them and then acting. This alternative is to recognize and then refuse "a world in which murder is legitimatized and where human life is considered futile. This is the prime political problem of today."[18]

The alternative, of refusing to legitimatize murder, cannot be accused of being Utopian. To the contrary, it is the only realistic attitude to take in face of the conflicting Utopian schemes which are trying to force themselves into reality. The arguments for continuing this struggle for Utopias are put forth so strongly

only because the people who present them are not able to imagine what death is for others. This is a characteristic of our century. Even as love is made over the telephone and work is done on a machine rather than matter, one kills and is killed today by proxy. There is an increase in cleanliness, but a loss in knowledge.[19]

Camus is pessimistic as to the outcome of this conflict of ideologies; he believes that we cannot reasonably hope that all will be saved, but, he says, in a highly revealing sentence, we can at least attempt "to save the bodies so that a future remains possible."[20] The importance of this phrase is that it reveals the substance of Camus' thinking about human nature. How can the future be assured through the saving of the bodies of men? The answer is left hanging by Camus, but the obvious inference, which is consonant with his whole thought, is that *human nature is basically physical*. Actually, there could be no other answer in terms of Camus' position: if there are no transcendent values, but yet values exist for man, then the source of these values must be in a given structure of man which is physical. This is not only consonant with Camus' philosophy but is an essential idea for an anti-theistic, constructive, moral philosophy. This idea would hold that within the complex of man's emotions and feelings there lies the basis for man's proper intellectual response to life, and, by extension, there lies the basis for man's revolt. The idea of revolt is not fully explicable without this presumption, for here in the physical life of men there is a nature which is on-going, imperative, and commonly held. We should recall the references in the early sections of *The Myth of Sisyphus* to the "habits of the body" which influence our decisions as strongly as our intellectual convictions. In *Noces* we find much fuller reference to this in Camus' discussion of the passion with which the Algerians live on the beaches, sunbathing in near nudity. This is the first time in two thousand years, since the athletes of Delos, that men have refound the importance of the body. This passion to live near bodies and by the body "has its nuances, its life, and, to hazard a bit of nonsense, a psychology which is its own. The evolution of the body, like that of the mind, has its history, its returns, its progress, and its deficit."[21] It is unfortunate that Camus does not enlarge upon this idea in his journalistic piece; it is a basic premise of his thought with much grounds for justification, and it is possible that in the coming years he may develop this premise if he moves toward a greater systematization of his philosophy.

In the two pieces, entitled "Mystified Socialism" and "The Travesty of the Revolution,"[22] we find a critique of Marxist-socialism with which we are, at this point, largely familiar. A moralistic socialism, contends Camus, cannot be reconciled with Marxism. The latter holds that any means are justified by the final communist society, whereas the former attempts to say that some means are not justified. Marxism, in this light is either absolutely true or absolutely false, inasmuch as its structure rests upon absolute prophetic claims. In relation to Marxism the question of the legitimacy of murder comes to a decision between an all-justifying end or a concern with limited goals and ends. Only in the latter choice can the time of ideologies be brought to an end. This choice cannot be suspended in hope of improvement through the "revolutions" which are proposed; revolutions, as a national movement for betterment, no longer exist. Revolution today is an international affair signifying the extension of one ideological empire and the retrenchment of another. To hope for revolution is to give in to the murder which it entails, for revolution is no longer a hope but is an instrument in the battle of Utopias which threatens us all. The alternative of refusing to legitimatize murder and of rejecting absolute goals means that we accept the *status quo*, or, as Camus terms it, we espouse a "relative Utopia" which is the "only possible and which is the only one to be inspired by the spirit of reality."[23]

The "reality" which Camus believes substantiates the proposal of a relative Utopia is discussed in the articles, "International Dictatorship and Democracy" and "The World Moves Quickly."[24] Here the thesis is that nations operate on an anachronistic basis in acting in terms of nationalities and frontiers. The basis for isolation no longer exists: all life, suffering, and tragedy are internationally collective. Nations must come to terms with this reality which makes obvious the need for international political and economic unity. We are moving toward a new order, which in part recognizes this need, but there are two ways in which this new order can be achieved. Either world unity will come from above by a single state, such as Russia or the United States, after a war in which millions will die for the happiness of the survivors; in this case the means for achieving unity in effect destroy the goal of universal happiness. Or else world unity will come through mutual accord. This second alternative, Camus feels, is possible principally because it is the only way possible of fully achieving the goal toward which the world is quickly pushing us. Mutual accord would mean an international democracy superior to national dictatorships, whether this be formulated through means of the United Nations or in some other form. This is the relative Utopia which can save us from the total war which anachronistic national policies are preparing. The choice is in accepting or rejecting the method of achieving unity through destruction.

If it is accepted, one should recognize himself as consciously responsible for the war to come. If it is rejected, one should either declare himself a partisan of the *status quo* . . . or else renew the content of the word "revolution" which constitutes an acceptance of what I shall term the relative Utopia.[25]

In the two final articles of the series, "Neither Victims Nor Hangmen," Camus suggests the program which he feels is best able to realize the relative Utopia.[26] He makes an appeal to both laboring and intellectual groups to establish on an international scale the bonds of a common attitude of mind and devotion to peace. A movement for mutual accord cannot be made through national governments which only operate in terms of national sovereignty and ideology. Articulate groups within nations must by-pass their national regimes and form a common international commitment to peace which, through its universal character, can force its governments toward mutual accord. This eminently sensible and persuasive proposal is a direct application of Camus' concern with revolt. Such a proposal is tantamount to a common revolt of all people against their national governments in the affirmation of their own common unity. This would "renew the content of the word 'revolution' " by linking it once more to its source, i.e., revolt. In face of the official confusion which characterizes national regimes, Camus appeals to intellectuals to pronounce clear judgments to the effect that world unity is the only problem that should challenge us if we are realistic in our thinking. The future, in effect, depends on clear reasoning to unravel the irrational knot of historical logic which strangles us, although this does not mean that we can do without the forces of love and indignation. Once again then, it is a question of reflecting and then choosing for or against silence, fear, enslavement, injustice, and falsehood. It is a question whether we shall revolt and affirm the value of universal communication between men. But Camus is not under an illusion as to the possibility which such a plan has for success. Even though this be the only efficacious and morally satisfactory program for the future, there is but the slightest of chances it shall be realized. But be this as it may, Camus feels that the choice to refuse the legitimatization of murder is morally incumbent upon us, so as to mark off one group of voices from those who do not refuse murder.

Since this terrible division exists, the clear delineation of it will at least be a step forward. Over five continents and through the years to come an interminable struggle is going to take place between violence and predication. And it is true that the chances of the first are a thousand times greater than those of the latter. But I have always thought that if the man who had hope in the human condition was a madman, he who despaired of history was a coward. And henceforth, the sole honor will be to hold obstinately to this tremendous wager which will finally decide if words are stronger than bullets.[27]

This series of editorial pieces is an example of the positive moral relevance which Camus' philosophy of limits has for contemporary issues. It is not caught in the indeterminate search for middle principles which attempts to reflect an abstract value such as "goodness." The consciousness of the solidarity of men in a common nature is, in itself, an undergirding value and middle principle all at the same time. The positive expression of this attitude shows Camus to be a nonconformist of a radical nature. His proposals cut roughshod

across most of the contemporary world's institutions and ideologies. From a national point of view his ideas are clearly
seditious. From a bourgeois point of view he is dangerously
radical. He has been roundly attacked by Christians, Marxists,
and existentialists. Yet there is great integrity to his thought
if we understand it in its total development. It is easy for his
critics to throw his mature thought against his earlier writings
and attempt to pass off his philosophy as lacking in consistency
and cogency, but it is less easy for them to meet his assertions
on a common ground. The many extreme reactions that we
find to the philosophy of Albert Camus are due in most part
to the fact that few have attempted a careful study of the
central concerns and convictions that motivate his thought.
Certainly this is true of Marxist scholars and communists
who persistently accuse Camus of giving solace to the injustice
of bourgeois society when he attacks the ideological foundations of the Soviet state. After defending himself from two
such attacks on the part of Emmanuel d'Astier de la Vigerie[28]
and Pierre Hervé,[29] it is understandable why Camus reacted so
indignantly when the same accusation was made on the part of
Francis Jeanson in Jean-Paul Sartre's *Les Temps Modernes*.[30]
This led to the famous, but rather unimportant, "break" between Camus and Sartre. The latter, in approving publication
of the article, allowed the twice-posed accusation of having
strong bourgeois sympathies to be put once again to Camus.
Jeanson's critique is not without some merit, but it commits
the oft-repeated error of fusing together the early and later
phases of Camus' thought to the end that Camus is to be
shown not only opposed to revolutions but to history itself.
Inasmuch as Camus is absolutely serious in his concern for
the oppressed, and inasmuch as *Les Temps Modernes* was the
most widely influential of French journals, Camus felt it
necessary to compose an extensive rebuttal to this charge.
Sartre took the occasion to make a somewhat dramatic and
formal break with Camus, though, as was mentioned earlier,

neither Camus nor Sartre ever claimed affinity for their respective positions.

The discussions and polemics which have arisen between Camus and Christian writers have been frequent. There is hardly a major piece of writing to come from the pen of Camus which has not made some reference to the Christian faith.[31] This is because Camus is probably the finest example of the *homme révolté* which he has described. He is in revolt against any man or institution which justifies its actions on the basis of eternal values, revelations, or divine mandates, and his accusation of the Christian faith rests on the values of justice, freedom, and human happiness. Christian thinkers are greatly attracted to Camus because of his constant preoccupation with religious concerns. Camus' rejection of the Christian faith is in part that of Ivan Karamazov, and also because he understands that the Christian attitude is one of resignation to the evil which is in the world, an evil over which the Christian triumphs not in this world but in another. Camus has remarked that the Christian faith is founded on an acceptance of injustice which does not find its resolution in this world, i.e., the crucifixion of Christ which finds its final resolution in the transcendent. For him, the essence of Christianity is its condemnation of this world for another and nonexistent world, which thus leaves the earthly misery of men unresolved. In both *The Stranger* and *The Plague* the figure of the priest plays the important role of providing a well-articulated answer to the problems of death and evil; it is this answer which Camus attempts to show dramatically to be in an insufficient response to men's immediate anguish when faced with evil and death. Whether Camus has done justice to the Christian faith in characterizing it as other-worldly is a matter which might be disputed by some, but, in any event, the questions which occupy Camus are those which occupy Christian theologians and philosophers, and Camus' response to these questions stands in a clear relief to those of Christians. We should not make the mistake of identifying Camus, like Kierkegaard, in a prophetic relation to the Church; the prophet calls the Church back to its essential nature from which it has strayed; Camus, to the contrary, calls the Church away from its essential nature and demands that it accept the human condition and the limited values which it holds.[32]

It should be evident, then, that the political thought of Albert Camus is nonconformist and holds itself in a position of judgment over the nihilist, terrorist, and conformist extremes which characterize the 20th century. It is a judgment which draws its strength from values found in the human condition itself, values which are articulated for the rest of mankind by the revolt of the oppressed against that which threatens these values. Revolt has revealed not only a common human nature but also the limits which seem to adhere in this nature. To more aptly describe the character of this human nature Camus has chosen the word *"mesure"* by which he intends "proportion" or "balance." It is at this point that we see more clearly the affinity which his thought shows for a Heraclitean worldview.

If the limit discovered by revolt transforms everything, if all thought, all action which goes beyond a certain point negates itself, then there is a proportion of things and of man. In history, as in psychology, revolt is an irregular pendulum which swings in the wildest arcs, because it is seeking its profound rhythm. But this irregularity is not complete. It functions around a pivot. At the same time that it suggests a nature common to all men revolt brings to light the proportion and limit which are at the principle of this nature.[33]

The concept of proportionality and the analogy of the pendulum are the interpretive ideas that we have been seeking throughout the historical analysis of revolt and revolution; the "wildest arcs" in which revolt has swung can be rationally comprehended only through the concept of human nature's proportions. The revolt of the past two centuries is not to be explained as madness, degeneracy, or sin; it is to be explained and justified by the enduring principle of human nature around which it has pivoted and sought.

The concept of human nature's proportionality is perfectly consonant with the whole development of what we have called the authentic thought of Albert Camus. But in presenting this term Camus briefly suggests a startling and quite unexpected idea. Note that he speaks of "a proportion *of things* and men." We may ask, "What things?", for Camus has not up to this point discussed the universe which surrounds men; he has been solely concerned with men in history. The concept of proportionality has, without warning, been applied to the world, and Camus invokes the authority of "science" in support of this concept, i.e.,

All reflection today, nihilist and positivist, sometimes without knowing it, gives birth to this proportionality of things that science itself confirms. Up to the present time the quantum theory, relativity, and the indeterminate quality of inter-relationships define a world which has a definable reality only on the scale of average greatness which is our own. The ideologies which guide our world were born during the time of absolute scientific truths on a grand scale. Our real knowledge, to the contrary, can only justify a system of thought based on a scale of relative dimensions. . . . Approximative thought, alone, is creative of reality.[34]

Then he goes on to add that

not even the very forces of matter, in their blind movement, can avoid imposing upon themselves their proper proportions.[35]

Only in those passages just quoted does Camus suggest that the concept of proportionality may be a universal principle and not simply a principle of human nature; after this he remains silent. In his desire for some more conclusive support for this principle, he has affirmed what, up to this point, he has denied, i.e., the presence of an order in the world which accords with the order in human nature. In briefly suggesting this idea and then dropping it, Camus demonstrates an interesting carelessness; interesting, because it shows that Camus' thinking is moving toward a more general and systematic philosophy; careless, because it is sharply incongruous with the authentic body of his thought and totally incongruous with the ideas of the *raisonnement absurde*. It was indicated at the close of Part One that the authentic thought of Albert Camus does not posit a total divorce of man from the world; that the "benign indifference of the universe" felt by Meursault and the strange fascination of nature felt by the youth in *Noces*, that these things indicated a certain acceptance of the world as humanly meaningful. The authentic thought of Camus includes the possibility of a positive reconciliation of man with the world, but this is a possibility which, at this point, has not been developed by Camus, and is therefore unfounded. That such an error should appear in his mature works does not detract from the value of his thought but only serves to emphasize the developing character of his philosophy, which at all times contains the possibility of surpassing itself by a partial negation in the achievement of a larger synthesis.

Within men and their history the law of proportion is that which controls history and gives action its value or disvalue. This law applies itself to all the paradoxes within which rebel thought moves, i.e., destruction or conformity, justice or freedom, violence or non-violence, rationality or reality. On the latter, the law of proportion teaches us that reality is not completely rational, nor is the rational completely real; alone, neither is sufficient, but together the irrational elements of reality limit the rational and give it its proper proportion. In a rare metaphysical statement Camus applies the principle of proportion to the question of being and becoming, i.e.,

Being can test itself only in becoming; becoming is nothing without being. The world is not in a state of pure fixity, but at the same time it is not solely movement. It is movement and fixity. The historical dialectic, for example, does not indefinitely pursue an unknown value; it moves in the orbit of limits which is the primary value.[36]

The principle of proportion shows itself to be a mediating value capable also of clarifying the moral antinomies of modern times. It shows us that virtues cannot be separated from reality without eventually becoming principles of evil. In the same way, virtues cannot be totally determined by history without eventually denying themselves. The value found in revolt is neither above history, as were Jacobin virtues, nor in history as the 20th century revolutions would have it; it is found in the experience of men in revolt who realize that every moral system must be, in part realistic, and that every realistic attitude must be, in part, moral.

This principle of proportion finds its seat in the lives of individual men; its function of mediating between extreme possibilities thus means that it is man himself that bears the tension between these extremes. There is no moral comfort for man. In recognizing the proportions of life he takes upon himself the tension, uncertainty, and risk which this recognition implies. Only in this tension will the value of revolt be preserved. "In a sense, on my self alone rests the common dignity which I cannot allow to be debased either in myself or others."[37] Camus maintains that, once born, revolt must continue in man, lest the condition against which he revolted return again. Revolt is not spasmodic, it is continuing, and in this continuing tension values are created and preserved. Values are not given; they are conquered in the struggle of individuals, e.g.,

There is no ideal freedom which will suddenly be given to us one day, like a pension which one receives at the close of his life. Freedoms are to be conquered one by one, painfully, and those which we already possess are the milestones, insufficient to be sure, on the way to a concrete liberation. If one allows them to be taken away, there is no advance. To the contrary, one moves backward, and one day it will be necessary to take this route over again, but this new effort will once more be brought about by the sweat and blood of men.[38]

In another place Camus makes the similar statement that

truth, like love and intelligence, is to be constructed. Indeed, nothing is given or promised, but all is possible for him who accepts to undertake and risk.[39]

According to this type of thought, the only individuals who advance history are those who can revolt against it; this is a thought reminiscent of Camus' early esthetics where he says that an artist creates best when he is able at any moment to give up the whole enterprise: a parallel which shows how greatly different is his mature philosophy from his absurdist meditations. In the earlier thought creation is meaningless; in the later thought it is the construction of meaning. The difference lies simply in the principle of revolt.

In the closing pages of *L'Homme révolté* Camus remarks that the preoccupation with the balance and proportion of life is a characteristic of the Mediterranean spirit, which stands in contrast to the historical absolutism typical of German and later Christian thought. The tradition of Mediterranean thought, which Camus calls *"la pensée solaire,"* holds nature to be an object of contemplation, not history. When nature is no longer contemplated and admired, it can only become the basis for its own transformation in the name of history. This is the struggle in which Europe has always been caught, i.e., that between the needs of human nature and the cause of historical absolutism. For Camus, it is the struggle between noon and midnight. It is with these things in mind that Camus characterizes his philosophy of limits as *"la pensée du midi."* "Midi," in this instance, is rich in meaning: the *midi* is the south and the whole Mediterranean world from which Camus speaks; midi is the noon with all that this implies of brightness, clarity, lucidity; Camus is conscious as well that the word, *midi,* echoes the "Great Noon" of Friedrich Nietzsche.

La pensée du midi envisages a world in which there will never be a final triumph over evil. This is why it calls man to a ceaseless revolt against the evil in life. In revolt and its limits we shall find not optimism but wisdom: the only efficacious wisdom for today. In his struggle with the evil that threatens him from without and the tension that burdens him from within, the rebel creates the values which make civilization. The struggle is endless; even after man has put forth his greatest effort there will still be suffering, injustice, and the death of innocent children. Man in revolt can arithmetically reduce evil in the world but never eradicate it. The scandal will yet remain, and the struggle will yet be necessary. Camus would probably say that without this struggle man would not be man, and unless he accepts this tension and struggle he does not fully realize his vocation as a man. Man is "that force which always ends by counterbalancing tyrants and gods."[40]

It is now the 20th century, says Camus, and neither divine nor revolutionary parousias have come. The only course open to man is revolt and the creation of his own world and his own values within the limits imposed upon him by his own nature. In this way civilization can be assured.

Revolt is not in itself an element of civilization. But it is antecedent to all civilization. In the impasse in which we live, it alone permits the hope for the future of which Nietzsche dreamed: "In place of the judge and represser, the creator."[41]

CHAPTER VIII
THE ESTHETICS
OF REVOLT

THE esthetic theory of the philosophy of limits merits special attention for at least two reasons. The first would be because it is an expression of this philosophy in its pure state. If there was some lack of clarity in the concept of revolt when studied in its historical context, this failing disappears when revolt is studied in an esthetic context. In the consideration of Albert Camus' earlier absurdist esthetics we observed that because of Camus' dual role as *littérateur* and philosopher his esthetic theory was the crucible for his general philosophical position; elsewhere he might take the liberty of being imprecise, but when his role as an artist was in question he must perforce be precise. This observation is equally true in regard to his philosophy of limits; we shall discover here a conception of revolt which may have gone partly unnoticed until this time.

A second reason for devoting special attention to the esthetics of revolt is that it stands in clear contrast to the absurdist esthetics and is largely contradictory of it. If it be true, then, that Camus' esthetics is the clearest expression of his philosophical position and also true that the later esthetics contradicts the earlier, then we should find at this point the clearest expression of the differences between the early and mature philosophy of Albert Camus.

Camus, himself, has made clear the preciseness which esthetics requires of his thought in this statement, i.e.,

Art also is this movement which exalts and denies at the same time. "No artist tolerates reality," says Nietzsche. This is true; but no artist can do without reality. Creation is demand for unity and refusal of the world. But it refuses the world because of what it lacks and in the name of what it sometimes is. Revolt can be observed here, outside of history, in a pure state with its original complication. Art, then, should give us a final perspective of the content of revolt.[1]

When Camus states that creation is "demand for unity and refusal of the world" he provides a root definition of revolt and the key to his thinking in both the historical and esthetic fields. It is Camus' thesis that in all revolt there is a metaphysical demand for unity which, going unsatisfied by the conditions of the world, attempts to build a universe which will satisfy this demand. It is revolt that creates universes, and, as Camus understands it, this is the key to understanding metaphysical revolt, revolution, and artistic creation. The demand which revolt makes is, in part, an esthetic demand.

All of the rebel philosophies studied by Camus in *L'Homme révolté* attempt to create a substitute universe which possesses the unity which they demand. They fabricate unity either through rhetoric or through the description of a closed universe. The ramparts of Lucretius, Sade's isolated castles, the romantic islands and rocks, Nietzsche's lonely climes, and also the prisons, the concentration camps, the intrenched nations, the empire of free slaves—all of these are expressions of the need for unity felt by rebels and revolutionaries. In a closed universe they are able to find human unity and knowledge. This fabrication of unity is the goal of the artist as well.

The artist remakes the world after his own fashion. The symphonies of nature do not have a measured rest. The world is never silent; its very quietness repeats the same notes eternally according to vibrations which escape us. As for those that we perceive, they are sounds, rarely a harmony, never a melody. Evenso, music does exist where symphonies are completed, where melody gives its form to the sounds which, alone, do not have it, where a particular arrangement of notes draws from natural disorder a unity which is satisfying for the mind and the heart.[2]

This is a description of the world which is consonant with the authentic thought of Camus, and, in truth, it is hardly removed from the youthful impressions of the world recounted in *Noces*. In part, this is the universe seen by Nietzsche: eternally repetitious, whose features and movements are governed by "vibrations which escape us." But, unlike Nietzsche, Camus cannot give himself to the world in the worship of a deified cosmos. This universe is unlike man, it is strange to him and unsatisfying. And man has it within him to reform the image of the world until it is satisfying to his own demand for unity. It is not a question of renouncing the world; it is a question of refusing its disorder and fabricating order and unity in its place, whether this be in one's own life, in the societal life, or in art works.

Sculpture, for example, does not attempt to depict reality as such, but seeks to stylize that reality. Resemblance is necessary, but this is not what is sought; the goal is to capture a gesture in the movement of reality which sums up all of the transitive gestures of life. Sculpture is successful when it imprisons concretely that in a body or a face which survives change and degradation.

In painting, as in sculpture, the essential task is to choose, isolate, and generalize that aspect of reality which is the subject. The first act of the landscape or still-life painter is to isolate in space and time that which exists as part of a larger universe of movement and transiency. The style which the painter imposes upon reality involves picturing a conjunction of nature and history, the imprisonment in the present moment of that which is always becoming. The sun-flower of Van Gogh or the landscape of Corot indeed look like the flowers of Arles or the shaded lakes of the Ville d'Avray, but the flower or lake on this canvas does not exist; it cannot be found in reality. Part of that reality has been negated so that unity could be found. Thus, the "style" which the artist imposes on reality is the result of his negation, and the greater the negation, the stronger will be the effect of the style. In times of great revolt artists stylize more strongly than when reality is accepted as unobtrusive and satisfying. Art is essentially a protest against what is and the attempt to replace this with the value which revolt demands. Hence, art as well as history has its times of extreme revolt when negation of the "what is" is carried to radical limits. But no art, nor any revolution, can live on a total negation of existent reality in the name of a value or vision which are beyond man's historical existence. The two terms of revolt limit us to a partial refusal of the world and a partial exaltation of its other features. "Thus, art takes us back to the origins of revolt in the measure in which it attempts to give form to a value which flees in perpetual becoming but which the artist grasps and desires to snatch from history."[3]

In the novel it is even more clearly seen that revolt is the motivating factor. Ancient literature, proceeding from a sacred universe, is a literature of consentment; the reality of life is accepted as eternally given, and so, within this consentment, literature functions only as a chronicle of historical crises and daily events. The novel is a product of the revolt of the last two centuries in which man defies God by creating his own history. The novel is rebellious because it refuses reality. It is not an evasion; it is the obstinate effort to refuse the world as it is, and, through its recreation, to find man's destiny therein. This nostalgia which drives men to impose unity on life is obvious in the most commonplace happenings. For example, every man enviously reads into the life of another a coherence and unity which are not, in fact, there. In the same sense, all men attempt to make their own lives works of art by struggling to make love, or a principle, or an attitude the ever enduring principles of their lives. The frustration of men comes from their discovery that nothing has duration. The desires of love and possession are in reality the desire to make things last as they are, to render all things forever sterile and perfect. This frustrating struggle of men is their revolt against the lack of duration. They seek endlessly to give a lasting form to a reality which will not remain still. Camus feels that it is elementary to say that all persons have an idea of what would be a unified and better world, and that all human actions seek to give life a form which it does not possess. This is precisely what the novel does: it creates a world which is not necessarily more beautiful, but which has unity, destiny, and completeness. It achieves this by correcting the world, and the unity which it gives to the world is the positive content of the artist's revolt.

Even as historical and metaphysical revolt have their extremes which overemphasize one or the other of the terms of revolt, the novel also presents this tendency. As illustrations of this, Camus cites the American novel of the twenties and thirties and the Proustian novel. The American novel follows the extreme of too completely accepting the reality of "what is" by reducing the figure of man to a series of unexplained acts and movements. This cannot be called "realism," because reality is here degraded to the point that all is on the same level, a feature which reality does not possess. To be faithful to reality does not mean depicting simply its outer "bark"; it means finding and completing a unity which runs through the interior of this reality. Camus is more attracted to Proust's effort to employ reality as the brute matter for the construction of a closed and intensely personal universe. In Proust the transient events of the exterior of life find their unity only in terms of certain unforgettable instances of the interior personal life. Camus feels that Proust's revolt is creative, because he has created a human unity out of the constant movement of forms by means of memory and intelligence.

The two extremes which Camus suggests are those of formal art and realist art. The former attempts a total negation of reality and the latter attempts its total acceptance, both of which are impossibilities. Both are absurd positions which desire to create unity where it cannot be found, i.e., in isolation from either principles or reality. True formalism, thus understood, could only be silence. And true realism would be interminable description. Between these two extremes the philosophy of limits asserts its mediating position. Revolt teaches us that in art unity is found only in the stylization of reality, and the greatest artistic style is the expression of the highest revolt. "When the most anguished cry finds its tautest language, revolt satisfies its true requirement and draws creative strength from this fidelity to itself."[4] The greatest style issues from the extreme tension of man's nostalgia and reality's disorder. Thus, the "demand for unity and refusal of the world" is the key description of the dynamics of revolt as well as of artistic creation.

If we think back at this point to the esthetic theory expounded in *The Myth of Sisyphus* we realize the distance which separates the absurdist experiment from the philosophy of limits. It was in this earlier work that Camus had said, "For the absurd man, it is no longer a question of explaining or resolving, but of feeling and describing. All begins with a clearvisioned indifference. To describe: this is the ultimate ambition of absurd thinking."[5] The esthetic injunction of the absurdist experiment was to describe the world with *nothing added to it*. This, of course, is not the case of the esthetics of revolt, for in the philosophy of limits Camus describes both man and the world in terms clearly contrasting with his earlier thought. The world is no longer strange and intractable; it is now capable of transformation. And, more importantly, man does not hold his nostalgia for unity in defiance of the world, but, in revolt, he now aggressively seeks to transform the world in the image of revolt's value. It is interesting that in this earlier esthetics Camus' basic description of man and his unity, and the world and its disunity, is much the same as it is in his mature thought. The essential difference is that earlier there was no compulsion for man to create a world of unity and values in view of his own condemnation to die along with his values; in the philosophy of limits man is called to the creation of value and recreation of the world in spite of death. This change which occurred in Camus' conception of man is due to his discovery of the solidarity of men in their struggle against oppression. The movement is very clearly from the "I" to the "we," and in this movement the whole character of his philosophy was transformed, so that from a moral point of view it is not the same philosophy. We may surmise that he discovered revolt and the solidarity of men during his activities with the *Résistance,* or perhaps through identification with the plight of the Arabs of Algeria, or again perhaps through his sympathies with the struggles of the French working class from which he sprang. It is incidental as to how he discovered the dimension of revolt, but, in any case, it is obvious that the discovery came after he had ventured his absurdist experiment. With this larger conception the moral presuppositions of *The Myth of Sisyphus* were washed away, and the earlier moral gropings of *The Stranger* and *Noces* were picked up again and refined. That the esthetics of revolt is in a direct line of development from *Noces* and *The Stranger,* despite the absurdist experiment which intervenes, is made manifestly clear by recalling the passage in *Noces,* to wit, that "few people understand that there is a refusal which has nothing in common with renouncement."[6] The seeds of the philosophy of revolt were there from the beginning; it was but a matter of time and experiment before they were to find their full voice.

The esthetics of revolt is thus seen to be cleanly in accord with the general philosophy of limits; it is integral to this philosophy. It holds that art, as well as human action, can find a creative synthesis only through holding the extremes of refusal and consent in the hardest tension. It holds that both art and revolution in the 20th century have exhibited the same contradiction, i.e., they furiously deny reality through mutilation and terror. Only in revolt can the proportions be re-established by which a creative synthesis will emerge. The difficulty of such a task cannot be denied, inasmuch as the burden of this tension will rest in the hearts of individual men. But that it is difficult does not hinder the fact that such a balance is necessary for the future of civilization. Camus is convinced, for example, that labor, which now is purely productive, cannot in the future be separated from creativity. He is equally convinced that from this point onward art cannot be validly concerned with individual passions, but must seek to encompass the collective passion, i.e., the human condition.[7] Revolt affirms human solidarity and, consequently, there can be no creative art which does not move toward this oneness. If future civilization is to achieve a common dignity of all men we can no longer afford to give ourselves up to one or the other extreme in which the modern world has thrust us; silence will not reign between men so long as our refusal moves us to action and our demand for the unity of men and the world hinders us from destruction. "Creation is like civilization: it supposes an uninterrupted tension between form and matter, becoming and mind, history and values. If the equilibrium is broken there is dictatorship or anarchy, propaganda or formal delirium. In both cases, creation, which coincides with a reasoned liberty, is impossible."[8]

CHAPTER IX
THE LITERATURE
OF REVOLT

ON SEVERAL occasions Albert Camus has expressed his admiration for the works of Herman Melville. It is probable that this admiration has its center in Melville's *Moby Dick*, a novel whose lasting qualities stem from the double imagery which is suggested in the whale. The novel, *The Plague* (1947), and the play, *L'Etat de siège* (1948), are literary pieces which are structured on this device of the double image. In both instances the image used is that of the plague; the novel employs the symbolism of the plague in a very general sense, and the play uses the same symbol in a much more specific sense. That Camus should build a literary work on a double image is not surprising; it is consonant with the conception he has had of himself, from the beginning, as a novelist and playwright, i.e., that great literary works are the successful dramatic incarnations of general philosophical positions. We should insist, as we have done in discussion of the literature of the Absurd, that Camus' literary productions cannot be understood properly without knowledge of his philosophical position. He is not a novelist who also writes philosophical essays; he is a philosopher who also writes novels. Those who would attempt to infer his philosophical position solely from his literary works do damage to his philosophy and, in the end, gain but a confused understanding of his literary goals. It is for these reasons that, up to this point, there has been little use of the abundant supply of literary criticism which has been devoted to the novels and plays of Albert Camus. While we are considering the non-literary, philosophical elements in Camus' literary works it may be interesting to turn to certain literary critics in order to see what is their understanding of Camus, the writer. The eminent French literary critic, Pierre Néraud de Boisdeffre, indicates the philosophical character of Camus' plays and novels in remarking that

the weakness of Camus is that he translates the mixed passions of men into a too pure geometry. In his works of imagination Camus seems incapable of forgetting what his characters *represent* with the result that he does not incarnate them for what they are, namely, bodies and souls indescribably mixed.[1]

The influence of philosophical concerns, on the reality depicted in Camus' works, is marked even more strongly by Germaine Brée, i.e.,

The terseness of Camus' writing, its carefully calculated, almost laconic understatement and objectivity, can mask only temporarily the visionary quality of a world in which landscapes, situations, conversations, thoughts all come to us refracted through an inner medium which determines their form, their relation to each other, and their significance.

Camus' so-called limitations are not necessarily his shortcomings. As often as not they are, in fact, the boundary lines of his universe; they delimit it, marking off what is novel in his creation. They bear his signature and define his originality[2]

And on the same page she says, "The lucidity which sustains his fiction is far closer to the lucidity of hallucination or dream than to the mechanically rational lucidity for which it is often mistaken."

Michel Mohrt goes still farther in maintaining that Camus is not concerned to depict reality so much as he is to create myths, i.e.,

It has been said that *La Peste* is an allegorical novel. We should say, rather, that all the works of Camus are bathed in allegory, the natural atmosphere of poetry. God has been exiled from an absurd universe, to be replaced by a multitude of gods and heroes bearing such names as Wind, Sea, Plague, the Condemned, Don Juan. All of Camus' characters are "bright with myth" . . . The myth can be retold, reinterpreted in various ways; but the myth itself remains immortal. Meursault, Martha, Tarrou are characters on the order of Sisyphus. This is no township competition, but an Olympian rivalry. The city of Oran in *La Peste* becomes a fabulous city suspended halfway between the real and the imaginary.[3]

To judge from these last two testimonies Camus is a writer who denies the real more than he affirms it and is intent upon creating a world of "formal art" out of the movement of history. Having examined this type of appreciation of Camus' literary works, it is of interest to note the understanding which Rachel Bespaloff brings to these same works. She recognizes the symbolism which Camus employs but contends that the reason these double images are used is that Camus has no other way to remain faithful in authentically describing the human condition and, at the same time, to suggest the philosophical values which he relates to that condition. Thus, in her opinion, Camus' symbolism is the result of his obstinate realism.

A moralistic poet and not a lyric poet, not possessing the gifts of visionary imagination which creates myths and worlds, Camus traces the outlines and leaves us to decipher them.[4]

The gamut of partially and totally contradictory opinions seen here closely reflects the varying degrees in which these several critics were conversant with the philosophy of Albert Camus. It is fair to say that Néraud de Boisdeffre and Bespaloff are more familiar with this philosophical position than are Brée or Mohrt. These latter two critics apparently feel that the "real" Camus is found in his literary works, and they have, consequently, become enmired in the infinite images and secret meanings which characterize any great literary production. The practical lesson which emerges from this brief contrast of literary critics is this: the literary critic should consult

Camus' philosophical works before philosophically analyzing his plays and novels; and also, the general reader should consult Camus' philosophical works before approaching the philosophical analyses of literary critics.

Our study of *The Plague* and *The State of Siege* will content itself with a brief analysis of their philosophical content. The ideas with which they are concerned are familiar to us at this point and hence a lengthy study would be needless. Both works are quite clearly works of revolt; it is in this that they are more advanced, philosophically, than Camus' earlier literary works. The play, *Les Justes*, which has already been discussed in reference to Ivan Kaliayev and the 1905 terrorists, belongs equally to this literature of revolt, although it is specifically concerned with the notion of limits. Camus is fully conscious of the advance which he makes over his earlier works as evidenced by his remark that no one "will have the idea of disputing that, if there is evolution from *The Stranger* to *The Plague*, it is in the direction of solidarity and participation."[5] The general position which runs through *The Plague* and *The State of Siege* is aptly stated by Camus, i.e., "The world in which I live is repugnant to me, but I feel a solidarity with the men who suffer in it."[6] This statement, as well as these two works, are both of the period 1947-48 and expressive of the general notion of revolt in its early and only partially developed form. A third work, *The Fall* (1956), carries us far beyond this early notion of revolt.

THE PLAGUE: A NOVEL

Albert Camus' second novel, *The Plague*,[7] is generally felt to be his greatest literary creation and was greeted by some as the greatest novel in France since Andre Malraux' *La Condition humaine*, published some fifteen years earlier. If it be the best of Camus' literary works, it is also, in the view of

Pierre-Henri Simon, "The most anti-Christian of all his books, because it is the one which affirms in the clearest manner a pure humanism, a religion of human nobility without God and even against God."[8]

The novel is a chronicle of the events in the Algerian city of Oran during the period when a general epidemic of bubonic plague afflicted its people and closed its gates to the outer world. The narrator of the chronicle is Dr. Bernard Rieux who tells the story in third person although he is one of the central participants. The narration is quiet, matter-of-fact, and somewhat detached, e.g.,

> To some these events will seem quite natural; to others, all but incredible. But, obviously, a narrator cannot take account of these differences of outlook. His business is only to say: "This is what happened," when he knows that it actually did happen, that it closely affected the life of a whole populace, and that there are thousands of eye-witnesses who can appraise in their hearts the truth of what he writes.[9]

It soon becomes obvious that Rieux is the spokesman for Albert Camus. In a conversation with a reporter we learn that "the language he used was that of a man who was sick and tired of the world he lived in—though he had much liking for his fellow men—and had resolved, for his part, to have no truck with injustice and compromises with the truth."[10] Rieux is *un homme révolté*. Later, a second man links himself with Rieux as another rebel. This is Tarrou, who also is a spokesman for revolt, but, unlike Rieux, he is able to put this revolt into intellectual form as well as into action. A third important figure, for the philosophical dialogue undergirding the novel, is Father Paneloux, a Jesuit priest. Paneloux provides a consistent and well-articulated Christian response to the horror of the plague, a response which finds a larger meaning in the misery which falls on the city. There are other and thoroughly interesting characters in the narrative, but they do not center in the dialogue and need not concern us here.

A few dead rats, later many, and then a tide of rats die in the streets of Oran. A few persons are stricken with spots and swellings, then more, and finally there are reports of fever and death all over the city; the authorities recognize the epidemic for what it is: the plague. Oran is quarantined; its gates are closed and guarded, and its people are locked within, at grips with the unseen plague. For the people the plague means terror and death without reason or warning; it is incomprehensible and mysterious. In answer to this confusion Father Paneloux presents a sermon which constitutes the first instance in the chronicle that the plague is explained. Paneloux, in his sermon, says,

If today the plague is in your midst, that is because the hour has struck for taking thought. The just man need have no fear, but the evil-doer has good cause to tremble. For plague is the flail of God and the world is his threshing floor, and implacably He will thresh out his harvest until the wheat is separated from the chaff. There will be more chaff than wheat, few chosen of the many called. Yet this calamity was not willed by God. Too long this world of ours has connived at evil, too long has it counted on the divine mercy, on God's forgiveness. Repentance was enough, men thought; nothing was forbidden. . . . For a long while God gazed down on this town with eyes of compassion; but he grew weary of waiting, His eternal hope was too long deferred, and now He has turned His face from us. And so, God's light withdrawn, we walk in darkness, in the thick darkness of this plague.[11]

According to Paneloux, the plague is the city's condign punishment for its sin; the people are not innocent victims, they are guilty sinners before the judgment of God.

The reaction against this conception of the plague comes after the death of a child whom Rieux had desperately hoped to save. Rieux, Paneloux, Tarrou, and others stand by the bed of the child, watching his struggles, hopeful that a new anti-plague serum might be successful. They stand by helplessly as the child's resistance wears away. There are faint groans, then silence: the child is dead. Rieux leaves the bedside and quickly

moves toward the door with a strange look on his face. Paneloux, having some consolation to express to Rieux, attempts to
stop him as he walks out. "Rieux swung around on him
fiercely. 'Ah! That child, anyhow, was innocent, and you know
it as well as I do!' "[12] Outside, Rieux sits down on a bench,
and presently Paneloux comes up to ask why Rieux had been
angry. Rieux apologizes: "I'm sorry. But weariness is a kind of
madness. And there are times when the only feeling I have is
one of mad revolt." Paneloux replies, "I know. . . . That sort of
thing is revolting because it passes our human understanding.
But perhaps we should love what we cannot understand."
Rieux' reply is

"No, Father. I've a very different idea of love. And until my
dying day I shall refuse to love a scheme of things in which children are put to torture."
A shade of disquietude crossed the priest's face. "Ah, doctor,"
he said sadly, "I've just realized what is meant by 'grace!' "
Rieux had sunk back again on the bench. His lassitude had returned and from its depths he spoke more gently:
"It's something I haven't got; that I know. But I'd rather not
discuss that with you. We're working side by side for something
that unites us—beyond blasphemy and prayers. And it's the only
thing that matters."
Paneloux sat down beside Rieux. It was obvious that he was
deeply moved.
"Yes, yes," he said, "you, too, are working for man's salvation."

And when Paneloux starts to leave he looks troubled and
asks Rieux if he has not been convinced of his, Paneloux',
understanding of the plague. Rieux tells him,

"What does it matter? What I hate is death and disease, as you
well know. And whether you wish it or not, we're allies, facing
them and fighting them together." Rieux was still holding Paneloux' hand. "So you see"—but he refrained from meeting the
priest's eyes—"God Himself can't part us now."[13]

This word of reconciliation spoken by Rieux is not founded
upon a higher theology but on the human condition; the

struggle which this imposes upon men forms the undeniable common ground for their unity and dialogue. Rieux' revolt and fight against the plague has brought to the fore his awareness that men have a common solidarity against the oppression of their condition. The protest of revolt has been guided by its value toward this declaration of oneness with Paneloux. There is probably no clearer dramatic expression in Camus' works than this of the two terms which are operative in man's revolt.[14]

The effect of this conversation is evidenced in Paneloux' second sermon in which he seems to mollify the severity of the earlier sermon which perhaps "had lacked in charity."[15] Rieux, who heard the sermon, sums it up in the following way, to wit, "we might try to explain the phenomenon of the plague, but above all, should learn what it had to teach us. Rieux gathered that, to the Father's thinking, there was really nothing to explain."[16] This, then sharply indicates the movement of Paneloux' thought away from the level of myth and down to the common ground invoked by Rieux.

The positive statement of *la pensée révoltée* comes from Rieux' friend, Tarrou, a strange and tormented man who had spent his life as a revolutionary soldier of fortune all over Europe. In Tarrou's eyes the plague takes on a very general meaning: it is all that oppresses and murders men, and thus, it is not simply the evil of the world but also the evil of men, armies, and regimes. For years he had not realized that the plague existed, and that he was part of it, but one day the realization comes, i.e.,

"And thus I came to understand that I, anyhow, had had plague through all those long years in which, paradoxically enough, I'd believed with all my soul that I was fighting it. I learned that I had had an indirect hand in the deaths of thousands of people; that I'd even brought about their deaths by approving of acts and principles which could only end that way."[17]

This was what Tarrou revolted against; the principles which emerged from the revolt are then put forth, i.e.,

"Yes, I've been ashamed ever since; I have realized that we all have plague, and I have lost my peace. And today I am still trying to find it; still trying to understand all those others and not to be the mortal enemy of anyone. I only know that one must do what one can to cease being plague-stricken, and that's the only way in which we can hope for some peace or, failing that, a decent death. . . . So that is why I resolved to have no truck with anything which, directly or indirectly, for good reasons or for bad, brings death to anyone or justifies others' putting him to death."[18]

For Tarrou, the plague is a spiritual as well as a physical disease, but, unlike its physical counterpart, the spiritual plague can be fought off. All men are heir to it, but the best men are those who seldom lapse into it. "And it needs tremendous will-power, a never ending tension of the mind, to avoid such lapses."[19]

We may well wonder if Tarrou is not speaking of sin when he talks of "lapses." The plague is evil and sin is giving in to this evil. It is obvious that Tarrou, in speaking for Camus, *is* speaking of sin, but that *it is sin without God*. This is to say that, in Tarrou's thought, evil is of this world, man is of this world, and sin is against a value which is of this world. God in no way figures in the problem. The struggle in which Tarrou and Rieux are engaged is defined by the plague which moves through the human condition; it is this struggle which is of ultimate importance, because it concerns the ultimate ends of man: his life and his death. Paneloux himself has realized that in order to give oneself to this common cause, he must move away from transcendental certainties and into the uncertainties of the human condition. *The Plague* should leave us with no doubt that Albert Camus is a religious philosopher, and, at least in this novel, there are grounds for the statement made by Rachel Bespaloff that Camus is proposing a "de-Christianized Christianity."[20] This idea is given strong emphasis when Tarrou says,

"It comes to this," Tarrou said almost casually; "What interests me is learning how to become a saint."

"But you don't believe in God."

"Exactly! Can one be a saint without God?—that's the problem, in fact the only problem, I'm up against today."[21]

This, of course, is the problem which Camus is also up against and which was posed in essence by *The Myth of Sisyphus* with its question, "Can one live without appeal to sources beyond ourselves?" In *The Plague* Camus is able to go one step farther and pose the question of sainthood, because here he has a value foundation which he did not have in *The Myth*, i.e., revolt and solidarity. Camus was able to say yes to the question of *The Myth*, but in *The Plague* Tarrou's question goes unanswered. And this is significant, because a life of revolt would be contradictory to a life of peace and sainthood. It seems impossible that sainthood could be achieved through revolt; in Camus' terms, sainthood would mean the denial of reality in favor of the value of universal solidarity and, by consequence could only lead to an acceptance of the real evil in the human condition and a betrayal of revolt. Tarrou's query is the nostalgia which burns through all of Camus' writings: if there be no eternal reward, then can we find peace in the heart of revolt's tension and anguish? Though the question is left hanging, we know that, whatever the answer, revolt is our prime value and prime truth which cannot be forsaken.

In the midst of the sleepless vigils, the innoculations, the ambulance trips to the hospitals, the burials of the dead, in the midst of the city's struggle against the plague, Tarrou's life is also taken away. Rieux, who had found with this strange man a friendship he had never before known, is himself stricken with the contradictions and anguish which his struggle has invoked.

How hard it must be to live only with what one knows and what one remembers, cut off from what one hopes for! It was thus, most probably, that Tarrou had lived, and he realized the bleak sterility of a life without illusions. There can be no peace without hope, and Tarrou, denying as he did the right to condemn anyone whomsoever—though he knew well that no one can help condemning and it befalls even the victim sometimes to turn executioner—Tarrou lived a life riddled with contradictions and had never known hope's solace. Did that explain his aspiration toward saintliness, his quest of peace by service in the cause of others? Actually, Rieux had no idea of the answer to that question, and it mattered little. The only picture of Tarrou he would always have would be the picture of a man who firmly gripped the steering-wheel of his car when driving, or else the picture of that stalwart body, now lying motionless. Knowing meant that: a living warmth, and a picture of death.[22]

Rieux is left with memories and contradictions, still engaged in the task of healing and saving men from the plague. And at last the plague is lifted; it is not defeated: it suddenly leaves as mysteriously as it came. The gates of the city are once again thrown open, and Oran is part of the world and the sea. As the city rejoices, Rieux continues his never-ending rounds, and late in the evening he is at home, watching from his terrace the rockets which soar into the air as part of a municipal celebration. Rieux, at the end of the struggle, tries to understand what has happened and is happening to him, his friends, the people of Oran; he is attempting to gauge that "collective passion" of the plague-stricken and, in a larger sense, of humanity.

Cottard, Tarrou, the men and the women Rieux had loved and lost—all alike, dead or guilty, were forgotten. Yes, the old fellow had been right; these people were "just the same as ever." But this was at once their strength and their innocence, and it was on this level, beyond all grief, that Rieux could feel himself at one with them.[23]

These people were innocent and remain innocent. It is this constancy of the people that makes the plague so meaningless and so unjust: its terror descended upon them, ravaged them, and yet left them the same as they have always been. There is but one thing which we learn from the plague, and that is that "there are more things to admire in men than to despise."[24]

None the less, he knew that the tale he had to tell could not be one of final victory. It could be only the record of what had had to be done, and what assuredly would have to be done again in the never ending fight against terror and its relentless onslaughts, despite their personal afflictions, by all who, while unable to be saints but refusing to bow down to pestilences, strive their utmost to be healers.[25]

In the common struggle against the oppressive plague men have discovered their solidarity, and with this discovery they have learned compassion and sympathy. Thus it is for the modern world and particularly is it so for the Europe of the past few decades. The plague is unrelenting and never-dying, and, consequently, our revolting against it is endless. The passages which have been cited are but islands in the larger drama which Camus has depicted, but they are the moments of lucidity in the otherwise meaningless struggle against the plague. And in these moments the drama of *The Plague* shows itself to be integral with the thought of Albert Camus. As for the narrative, which has not been seen in this study, P.-H. Simon has the following to say, i.e.,

The sympathy for man who submits to his hard destiny with dignity, the pity for beings torn by suffering, the scandal of the death of a child, the anger against social oppression when it adds its cruelties to those of destiny—no where have these things found a form of expression which is at the same time fuller, more sober, and which has a like shock.[26]

That a work of such quietness and sobriety should possess an unequalled shock is the curious characteristic of Camus, the writer. In this respect, the novel, *The Plague,* is simply a corrolary of a philosophy whose "modesty" conceals the anguished and implacable probing of the ills which have overwhelmed an age. *The Plague* has opened itself fully to the ills of an age, has fully suffered them, and, in the end, has risen above them; it is for this reason that it is a classic of our time.

THE STAGE OF SIEGE: A PLAY

The Stage of Siege[27] is a play which uses the double-image of the plague to a much more concrete and more specific purpose than is so for *The Plague*. That it is more concrete is made evident in the play itself: the plague is here personified. That the meaning of the plague is more specific is best indicated by a statement made by Albert Camus shortly after the production of this play, i.e.,

... I did not seek to flatter anyone in writing *The State of Siege*. I wanted to attack directly a type of political society which has been organized or is being organized, to the right or to the left, on a totalitarian basis. No spectator can in good faith doubt that this play takes sides with the individual, in that which is noble in the flesh, in short, with terrestrial love, against the abstractions and the terrors of the totalitarian state, whether this be Russian, German, or Spanish.[28]

In this instance it happens to be Spanish. The place is the city of Cadiz. We should not be surprised that Camus has chosen Spain as the setting for one of his literary works, for we know that his mother was Spanish, and Camus, in the "Don Juan" section of *The Myth of Sisyphus* and in other writings, has shown the deep love which he holds for the Iberian peninsula.[29] *The State of Siege* was written in collaboration with Jean-Louis Barrault; it is highly unconventional, having the character of an allegorical morality play. Here we may in truth say that the reality of the characters is lost in the myth which they present; the myth of the plague was precisely what the two collaborators sought to portray.

A strange comet moves across the heavens, and the populace of Cadiz is terror-stricken, for a comet is an ill omen. Their fears as to what will happen are allayed by the governor who assures them that, in reality, they saw nothing. He ordains that "nothing happened." The people are reassured, and all is in order as it always was: they, as well as the governor, desire to negate change. But Diégo and the drunken Nada (which in Spanish signifies "nothing") do not believe that all is in order. Their premonitions are confirmed when, in the city square, a man suddenly drops dead. The doctors examine him and utter the dreaded word, "plague."

The terror which now possesses the people is allayed by the priest of the town in words which parallel those of Paneloux in *The Plague*, i.e., the plague is God's punishment for our sins.[30] Then, without warning, the Plague, himself, comes into the city, declares the governor deposed, and announces his own reign: the state of siege has begun. The Plague and his secretary, who has a name-list of all the city's inhabitants, establish their reign through the power of death which they have over all men. At the word of the Plague the secretary crosses out a name, and a dull sound indicates the death of that person. Death rules the populace, and the city's gates are closed to the outside world; the people are alone and faced with a struggle with death. The Chorus expresses the people's misery:

Woe! Woe! We are alone, we and the Plague! The last gate has closed! Nothing is heard any longer. The sea is henceforth too far away. Now we are in pain, and we shall circle about in this narrow city, without trees and without water, locked behind high, smooth gates which are topped by howling crowds, Cadiz is a black and red arena where ritual murders shall unroll. Brothers, this distress is greater than our fault, we have not deserved this prison! Our hearts were not innocent, but we loved the world and its summers: this should have saved us! The winds have failed and the sky is empty! We shall be silent for a long time. But one last time, before our mouths are closed with the gag of terror, we shall cry out in the desert.[31]

As part of his reign, the Plague has required that all citizens must carry "certificates of existence"; these are obtained after the citizen has answered the question as to why he should exist. Those who can little justify their existence, in the eyes of the new administration, receive low priority ratings for their existence and are placed at the top of the list carried by the secretary of the Plague. The goal of the new regime is to bring human destiny under control. Whereas, heretofore, the people died here and there in haphazard fashion and without any logic, now the people will die in an orderly and prearranged manner, with great logic and precision. Nor is difference and irrationality to be tolerated in the people; henceforth they shall be reasonable, and this is made possible through the numbering of each citizen and his placement according to priority. As the Plague sums up his reign, "I bring you silence, order, and absolute justice. I don't ask you to thank me, it being that what I do for you is quite natural. But I require your collaboration." Camus presents us with a mythical-dramatic example of what happens when the need for justice is absolutized to the neglect of freedom, i.e., what happens when revolt has been betrayed. The condemnation which the play carries for modern totalitarian societies is clearly specific in nature.

Even though here, as in *The Plague*, Camus has employed the same double-image, the mistake should not be made of equating the philosophical content of the two works. In the novel, the plague is that pervasive evil which ceaselessly afflicts men, and against which men can struggle, learn, and survive, but which they cannot defeat. In the play, however, the plague is a man-made totalitarian ideology and regime against which men can struggle and, eventually, defeat. The problem of the play is not the evil of the world and society, but, specifically, evil of a certain type of political society. In this specific area Camus asserts the position that man can triumph over the plague; he can do so through revolt which reasserts the original value which the plague of absolute justice has betrayed. The philosophical structure of the play is thus solid with the political theory which Camus' has presented in *L'Homme révolté* and in the editorial series "Neither Victims Nor Hangmen."

The revolt which defeats the Plague breaks forth in Diégo. He says to the secretary of the Plague,

I have well understood your system. You have given them pain, and hunger, and separations to distract them from their revolt. You exhaust them, swallow up their time and their strength so that they will have neither the leisure nor force of fury! Rest content, they are cowed! They are alone in spite of their mass, as I also am alone. Each of us is alone because of the cowardice of others. . . . Don't laugh. Don't laugh, imbecile. You are defeated, I tell you. In the midst of your most evident victories you are already defeated, because there is in man . . . a force which you will not reduce, a lucid madness, mixed with fear and courage, ignorant and victorious for all times. This is the force which is going to rise up, and then you will know that your glory was but smoke.[32]

Later Diégo expands his condemnation of the Plague into terms which are familiar in Camus' thought, e.g., he condemns the theory that one must kill in order to do away with murder, and that violence must be used to heal injustice; this is a centuries-old formula which the rebel rejects.[33] Diégo is not blind to the cowardice and cruelty of men, but this is no reason that they should be systematically controlled and oppressed. It is in recognition of men's weaknesses that Diégo is able to make the formula that "No man is so virtuous that one can grant him absolute power."[34]

The State of Siege, which was finished approximately a year after *The Plague*, shows a clear advance over the novel in its ideas concerning the nature of revolt. Not only are the two terms of revolt more sharply contrasted, but also we find the notion of "limits" which *The Plague* does not explicitly suggest. Hence, the play constitutes one of the earliest references to the idea which is later to place human revolt in the context of a philosophy of limits. In the closing moments of the play, after the Plague has been vanquished and the gates of Cadiz are about to open, the Chorus puts forth this new theme, i.e.,

No, there is no justice, but there are limits. And those who claim to regulate nothing, like those who intend to regulate everything, equally go beyond the limits. Open the gates, that the wind and salt may come scour this town.[35]

The "tension" which Tarrou had said was necessary in order to fight off the plague has become more clearly defined, and the concept of limits is the issue. It may be recalled that already, in *The Myth of Sisyphus*, Camus had presented this idea in reference to the Absurd, which, like revolt, is a human condition which is constantly upheld in the tension which either draws it into the nihilistic acceptance of the world or the monastic rejection of the world. The philosophy of limits could not arise out of this absurdist tension, because this tension was devoid of the "we" and of the conviction that in the solidarity of men there can be creation of values. Once this solidarity is discovered, then Camus is in the area of human values and conflict. Having to do with "men" rather than "man" the idea of tension and revolt re-emerges in a new form, and the creative concept of revolt and limits begins to develop. From this point onward a Heraclitian world-view is formed which has not yet reached its full development in the philosophy of Albert Camus. Whether a philosophy of proportion can be expanded to include the world as well as man is one of the central problems with which Camus' thought is faced. It would seem that a failure to do so would not detract from his philosophy of revolt, but if it were possible it would mean a degree of systematization which would strongly effect and clarify what is in the world as such that man revolts against. The thought of Albert Camus will continue to grow and surpass itself, but this growth will take place in a world which seems to have a proportional structure, a structure which Camus has indicated by Heraclitus' analogy of the bow, i.e.,

At this moment, when each of us must fit an arrow to his bow and enter the lists anew, to conquer, within history and in spite of it, that which he owns already, the thin yield of his fields, the brief love of this earth, at this moment when at last a man is born, it is time to forsake our age and its adolescent rages. The bow bends; the wood complains. At the moment of supreme tension, there will leap into flight an unswerving arrow, a shaft that is inflexible and free.[36]

THE FALL: A CONFESSIONAL NARRATIVE

To say that the thought of Albert Camus is a growing, self-surpassing activity does not simply mean it is changing and taking on new expressions and will continue to do so, never achieving finality. This quality of growth has to do as well with the very manner in which the complex of lyricism and thought gradually forms and develops a single, unified work. The growing character of Camus' thought is firmly rooted in his artistic temperament. And thus it is highly interesting to note that Camus' novels appear in every case to have been artistic leaps into a philosophical position which he was unable at that time to make clear. *The Stranger* presaged an outlook which was experimentally developed in *The Myth* and later corrected and defined in the "Remarque sur la révolte." *The Plague* added the possibility of a philosophy of limits which was not to become clarified until *L'Homme révolté*. It seems that Camus "feels" his way into philosophy. His thought takes on form in the gradual manner of a growing art-work. He moves forward through a kind of lyrical intuition which first finds its reality and validation in dramatic form. He thinks existentially before he thinks rationally, and this is the mark of an artistic temperament. This could be called a lyrical method in philosophy even as Camus himself can be most clearly described as a lyrical existentialist. Camus is, himself, fully aware of this quality about his thinking, and this is the final reason why he can admit to having a philosophy but not to being a philosopher, even as conversely this is the final justification for our saying that his art-works cannot be fully appreciated purely from an artistic viewpoint. The genius and power of his philosophy is that it has grown out of an artistic integrity which infuses this philosophy with a personal immediacy and applicability. And the wonder of his art works is that they are structured on a rationale of thought which carries beyond the confines of the work's immediate drama and points to an immensely wider realm in which this drama finds an ultimate meaning and universality.

It is because of this quality of Albert Camus as thinker and artist that his novels have tended to be harbingers of some coming extension or enrichment of his thought. The work, *The Fall*,[37] is just such a harbinger. It could hardly be called a novel, nor does Camus himself do so; for him it is a *récit*, a narrative. And in order to fix the work clearly we need only to add the remark that *The Fall* is a confessional narrative.

The Fall ranks easily in significance with the two earlier novels. But it is a different kind of work and one which must be read gently. It is a quiet narrative: it does not have the flash of the Algerian sun and the roar of a pistol echoing down white beaches, nor does it have the groaning terror of a city struggling under the unseen hand of death; its loudest sound is the distant splash of a young body as it plummets into the night-filled waters of the Seine. And one must listen with a sensitive ear if one is to hear the enormity of that innocent sound. The quietness itself of this work is deceptive, for at any moment the atmosphere of the narrative is so charged and tense that it could lose all sense of proportion and suddenly explode. Among the most striking features of Camus' novels has been the stylistic and dramatic control with which he has restrained and subdued his narrative; in this respect *The Fall* is a masterpiece, for nowhere else has his story been so tightly controlled. For that matter there is probably no work in recent fiction to compare with *The Fall* in this feature of putting enormous restraint on a narrative of such personal intensity. The rhythm of the story is never broken; only for a brief moment in the final scene does the movement quicken, threaten to break, and then catch itself once more.

But we said that this was a confessional narrative. The

confessor in this instance is Jean-Baptiste Clamence, noted
Paris defense lawyer who had attained fame, some fortune,
and considerable happiness as defender of society's unfortunate criminals and helpless oppressed. He was a pleader of
unusual lyrical and persuasive powers who played the role of
protector, interceding for the accused before the heartless
machinery of justice. Clamence was one of those blessed individuals for whom virtue was its own ample reward. Life offered
itself to him without restraint: he had position, respect, the
love of women, and the affection of friends. He was, by all
standards, not only a supremely happy man but an astonish-
ingly good man. But then, without apparent warning, he began
to change; quite deliberately he folded up the serenity of his
life and disappeared from Paris, from France, from all that he
had known and loved. He became of his own free will an exile,
a man withdrawn and set apart from the world that we know.

Clamence turns up in Amsterdam, and it is only by accident
that the reader, while slumming, meets him in one of those
bars with which European port towns are dotted: a motley
consort of world transients mixed with local thieves, prosti-
tutes, and procurers. Having forsaken all, he has taken refuge
with the accused and rejected of the world; he has come home
to the criminals and lost souls which he once defended. If
not of publicans, he is at least the friend of sinners. It is here
that we hear his narrative and come to appreciate the background of what has happened. Clamence tells us why it was
that he has fallen from the paradise he once knew.

Jean-Baptiste Clamence and his story constitute a remarkable event in the career of Camus. The story is remarkable in
three ways. One of these, obviously, is that Camus has for
the first time dealt directly and seriously not only with religious
symbols and myths but with religious problems themselves.
The ideas and problems of immortality, guilt, innocence,
judgment, christology, duty, and hope have, from the beginning, played a necessary yet subdued role in Camus' works;

they were problems which remained in the background while Camus turned his attention to immediate problems of a social nature. Even his frequent concern with teleology and the idea of God has been largely a concern for them as philosophical concepts having a bearing on social history. He has stylized the problem of God, dealing with it only in terms of what a certain conception of God (e.g., an Hegelian-Marxist conception) means for men when it is translated into political institutions. From the perspective which we now have of the total works of Camus it is clear that up until *The Fall* he has been busy developing and implementing the negative, prophetic side of his "revolt." And the whole gamut of religious problems was caught up negatively and only to the extent that they were implicated in the political scheme of things against which he protested. *The Fall* is highly significant in that it marks a change of concern to the religious problems implied in explaining the sources of human revolt and in understanding the life of creative revolt itself.

But a second and equally remarkable thing about *The Fall* is that it reveals Camus as a psychologist. For the first time he deals directly and seriously with the psychological make-up of men, especially contemporary men in their moral actions. The largest part of Clamence's narrative comprises thoughtful and acute observations on the peculiar motivations and justifications which men may have for their actions. Clamence's remarks are little psychological vignettes highly reminiscent of the short epithetical observations which characterized a portion of the early works of Nietzsche. With *The Fall* Camus seems to be moving toward a place with two other great religious-moral psychologists: Nietzsche and Kierkegaard.

The third remarkable quality about this story is that it is the most personal of all Camus' works; not even in *Noces* does Camus show such a conscious reflective concern for his own personal history. This, of course, is the real significance of the work as a confessional narrative: it is Camus himself who, very clearly, has raised his voice in confession. And it is just as clear (and this is the difficulty) that it is uncertain whose history and whose sins he is confessing. In no other work has Camus so enjoyed playing with his readers, alternately speaking rather obviously about himself and abruptly shoving the mask of Clamence between himself and the reader without so much as a comma or period of warning. In this regard surely none of his pages conceal so much playful irony as do those of *The Fall*. And the net result is that this, the most personal of Camus' works, is the least revealing. It seems that he is not concerned about adding to the Camus "legend" so much as he is to confound any attempt of others to build a legend around him. The problem of distinguishing the mask of Camus from the mask of Clamence is simply that we know, after a fashion, who Camus is, but we don't know who Clamence is. Certainly, in the description of the eloquent pleader for the accused and oppressed, the formidable opponent of judges and heartless legalism, we find a portrait of the Camus we know, indeed a self-portrait as astonishing as it is admirable in its self-deprecating honesty. And in many remarks and judgments we recognize what is too characteristic not to be about Camus. But what is left over—and this is the major portion of the work—is a figure who calls himself Jean-Baptiste Clamence, and even this is an assumed name which conceals rather than identifies the figure behind it. However, before the confession is out and the narrative done, Clamence reveals to his interlocutor the nature of the confession he has been hearing. He admits that

. . . I adapt my words to my listener and lead him to go me one better. I mingle what concerns me and what concerns others. I choose the features we have in common, the experiences we have endured together, the failings we share—good form, in other words, the man of the hour as he is rife in me and in others. With all that I construct a portrait which is the image of all and of no one. A mask, in short, rather like those carnival masks which are both lifelike and stylized, so that they make people say: "Why surely I've met him!" When the portrait is finished, as it is this evening, I show it with great sorrow: "This, alas, is what I am!" The prosecutor's charge is finished. But at the same time the portrait I hold out to my contemporaries becomes a mirror.[38]

Clamence, then, is "the image of all and of no one," the image of Camus and the reader, of you and I. And thus it is no curious coincidence that the interlocutor turns out to be a lawyer as was Clamence. The implication is that Clamence turns himself out to be a lawyer expressly for the occasion. On his next confession he might become a doctor, a teacher, or even a politician, all depending on whom he conversed with. Hence, this is not simply a confession of Camus, nor simply a confession of Clamence; it is simply a confession, a narrative whose particular elements are unimportant and flexible, and whose general elements are highly important and universally applicable. As in the earlier two novels, the moral import of the narrative has again carried far beyond the confines of the immediate story. Locked within this strange personal and yet universal confession are the existential sketches of a new growth in Camus' philosophy.

And so it is that *The Fall* is the harbinger of another extension in the thought and art of Albert Camus. We shall see, shortly, what a decisive reversal of concern is actually involved here. Yet, strange as it may at first appear, the work is neither unprepared nor out of character: it is authentic Camus. In it, Camus has, in a radical way, returned to himself, resigned himself to that difficult inner asceticism which is the heart of his revolt. The marked religious, psychological, and personal traits of the narrative simply display this return to self.

There is no need here to go over the myriad psychological and religious observations of *The Fall*, but there are some central moments in the narrative, and of these something must be said. The crucial event in Clamence's life in his Parisian "paradise" was the night when, returning home over the Pont Royal, he passed a girl who was leaning over the railing, staring into the river. It was one o'clock, and a drizzling rain assured the presence of no one else on the streets. There were but two people there: Clamence and the girl who stared into the Seine. When Clamence had crossed over the bridge and strolled eastward toward St. Michel he heard a splash and then a series of cries as the body was swept downstream. Clamence stopped and listened, knowing he should do something, yet realizing he wouldn't do anything. There was only himself and a being's cry of help. He listened there in the rain and the night, aware of the great distance between himself and the drowning girl, the swift current of the river, the coldness of the water, and the effort of the almost impossible attempt to rescue the girl. He was dimly aware of these things: they were in the back of a mind which was pleasantly becalmed by the exertions of an evening's love-making. The cry of the girl did not quite penetrate through the lethargy of Clamence's lingering self-enjoyment. He stopped, listened, and then walked on. It was too late then, too late for anything, for this was the beginning of his fall. When he ignored the cry and walked on he had given the lie to his entire life of virtue: here he was, completely alone and uncompelled before this distressed cry; he was, in that moment, perfectly free; and when his love for others was tested in that moment he discovered that he loved only himself, that his whole life of virtue and service to others was a sham, was nothing more than a means of buttressing his self-importance and sense of superiority. The distant splash of a young body into the night-filled waters of the Seine has, without his realizing it, commenced the destruction of Clamence. He will never again be the same.

The other central moment in Clamence's narrative is simply derived from this crucial event just recounted. It is the moment, two or three years later, when Clamence first becomes aware of his fall, and it occurs, quite understandably, on a bridge over the Seine. It is night, and Clamence again stands alone, this time gazing out over the river and sensing within him an overwhelming feeling of power and personal completion in this paradise which he has made so fully his own. At this moment he hears laughter behind him. He turns, but no one is there. The laughter breaks out once again, this time as if drifting downstream. But there is no one on the river; there is no one anywhere: there is just Clamence alone with the laughter. And it is this happening, which follows so naturally from the earlier incident on the Seine, which precipitates Clamence's fall, transforming him into the figure we meet in the Amsterdam bar, the judge-penitent who, by condemning his own life in the most general terms, is simultaneously condemning the life of his listener, is, in fact, provoking in his listener a process of self-judgment. Only by judging himself can he escape the judgment and mocking laughter of others and at the same time earn the right of judging others. Only in proclaiming the inescapable guilt of all men can Clamence lighten the burden of judgment which has weighed upon him. What is at stake in all this is a man's freedom. Clamence is telling us that men are free but that no man wants to bear the guilt which freedom must entail. The heart of his confession is that "on the bridges of Paris I, too, learned that I was afraid of freedom."[39] He had freely chosen to ignore the cry of distress but, in the end, he was unable to endure the personal guilt which this free choice brought with it. He was caught between social virtue and personal freedom, and his guilt showed him that in his inner being he was free even from morality. Clamence had neither God, nor confessor, nor master to whom he could give up his burden of freedom: no such messiah had yet come along. And in this interim period the one thing possible for this latter day John the Baptist was at least to proclaim the guilt of all men, thereby compromising the freedom which he knew he could never escape.

A very real question to interpose at this juncture is this: Which way has Clamence fallen, down or up? A man who has lost a paradise is presumably a man who has fallen "downward" and away from a higher state. But it so happens that the paradise of Clamence was not lost but was rejected, indeed, fled from. The prelapsarian Clamence was a man of blithesome, unconscious wholeness. His virtue gave direction to his being, sufficed for all, protected him from shock, reflection, or doubt. Clamence was indistinguishable from his habitual virtues until that crucial moment when the plaint of a drowning woman inserted itself between Clamence and his virtue. In that instant Clamence chose himself and not his virtue, he suddenly acted as a completely free individual and, in this very act, took upon himself the enormous, inescapable responsibility for his act. He was no longer safe or unconscious; he was in trouble. His virtue could not justify his action; he alone had to be its justification. From this point onward, Clamence moved toward consciousness and the agony of decision. In this respect Clamence did not fall downward but upward; he fell into a higher state: that of self-conscious freedom. All things told, he is morally more solid than he was previously. But the difficulty is that no matter how we view it Clamence has gone from one state to another neither through his own choice nor through the choice of another being. Whether one considers it a better or worse state is indifferent inasmuch as Clamence had suffered an experience which made his transformation unavoidable. Clamence forsook his "paradise" for the simple reason that he could do no other. He had discovered the burden of freedom, and this was his fall.

And in what way is Jean-Baptiste Clamence "the image of all and of no one?" In what way is he you or I, the picture of his times? We need only ask ourselves: In what way are we, children of the 20th century, like someone who could once act simply and innocently, never knowing the agony of moral uncertainty or the deep gnawing of freedom, because we were protected from this gnawing and this agony by the impassibility of the heavens, the assurance of revelation, the reassurance of providence, the divinely inspired rule of kings, and the divinely given word of the law? and in what way are we, children of the 20th century, like someone who has, through inexplicable events, lost this simplicity and innocence, having awakened to the consciousness of a freedom which gives lie to the pretension of providence and divine rule and leaves us heir to moral uncertainty and the gnawing of freedom? Clamence is a man in serious trouble, and the suggestion is that a whole age is in serious trouble. Clamence, as well as an entire age, has fallen out of one state and into another; both states of mind have their advantages and both have their drawbacks; it was neither an advance nor a decline. It was unavoidable: neither Clamence nor his age could help themselves.

This confessional narrative never goes beyond the point of being a confession: the rich anguish of Clamence and his age is methodically, if playfully, laid out before us and then left there. The narrative progressively charges the air with the weight of trouble and allows it to remain, trembling, without the dissipating breath of the ready answer which makes all things right. Camus has brought us trouble, a whole vision of trouble, and he has given us little more with which to deal with it than a certain irony and cynicism, and a searing honesty.

We have said that *The Fall* is a foretoken of some seachange in Camus' thought, and the truth of this appears obvious enough in just the manner in which Camus ends his narrative in an unresolved cynicism. The implacable lucidity of *The Myth* is not here to lead us into the open, nor do we find the impassioned argument of *The Rebel* which gives us a balanced perspective beyond the tangle of history. These previous high points of Camus' thought have no application here; he is no longer dealing with the romanticized individual facing a fragmented universe nor the rebellious individual facing an oppressive metaphysical or political system. For the first time Camus is concerned with the individual as he faces himself, i.e., the reflective individual attempting to bring his personal history and destiny into accord with his understanding of himself and his world. And this is what was meant in pointing out the novel religious and psychological qualities of *The Fall*. But, having noted this religious character of the work, we still cannot help being troubled by the unresolved quality of the narrative. One feels that "it is not quite Camus," that "it doesn't conform to type." The unrelieved tension and irony of *The Fall* appear bewildering and unaccountable to the admirer of Camus. And yet, what we wish to do from this point onward is to make it very clear that the genius and beauty of this work resides in the charged atmosphere which is left above us like a pall. To understand this peculiarity is to understand the narrative as a whole.

The first thing to note is that this unprecedented air of tense cynicism is not entirely unprecedented. Three years previous, in a short, sketchy shipboard diary,[40] Camus had already unveiled this curious attitude with the cryptic remark that there is

No homeland for the despairer and me, I know that the sea goes before me and follows me, I have a ready made folly. Those who love one another and are separated can live in pain, but this is not despair: they know that love exists. This is why, with dry eyes, I suffer exile. I am still waiting. A day will come, finally....[41]

And, almost as if in continuing, he writes later, i.e.,

Thus a day will come which will bring the completion of everything; hence it is necessary to let oneself go on and on like those who swim until exhaustion. The completion of what? From the beginning I have refused to reveal it to myself. Oh bitter bed, princely couch, the crown is in the depths of the waters.[42]

These are, of course, highly personal remarks and at the same time rather unusual words to have come from the pen of Camus. Yet it is significant enough that Camus wished to see such passages made public. The notions of exile, waiting, and an unknown, still unfulfilled destiny are woven about the central image of the sea and portray both here and throughout much of the shipboard diary the thinking of a man who chafes against his past and present and views the future with a strange and visionary hope. For Camus, the sea is always more than the sea; his love for it has brought with it a vaster love for that which is innocent, young, cleansing and, in a wider sense, redemptive. If Camus feels himself alienated from these qualities, it is not that he feels himself entirely alone in this. For him, an entire age is in exile from the beauty of the sea, and he has been content as a child of this age to reflect the anguish of that exile more sensitively perhaps than any other. And the difficulty is that this is not an exile which can be ended simply by wishing it. The exile from the redeeming beauties of life is not self-imposed either by Camus or his age. It simply happened. They "fell" into it, and now they must live it through. To deny it would be to deny the one reality that was given them: their present history. And yet to forget or ignore that state of youth in which the world's beauty is enjoyed innocently and fully, to forget this would be to take away that which makes this exile bearable and somehow filled with hope. If we understand the dialectic of anguish which flows from such exile then we can appreciate the awful poignancy of that moment in *The Fall* when Clamence, feeling the misery of his exile, allows the seams of this dialectic to stretch wide and almost burst, i.e.,

On the Damrak the first streetcar sounds its bell in the damp air and marks the awakening of life at the extremity of this Europe where, at the same moment, hundreds of millions of men, my subjects, painfully slip out of bed, a bitter taste in their mouths, to go to a joyless work. Then, soaring over this whole continent which is under my sway without knowing it, drinking in the absinthe-colored light of breaking day, intoxicated with evil words, I am happy—I am happy, I tell you, I won't let you think I'm not happy, I am happy unto death! Oh, sun, beaches, and the islands in the path of the trade winds, youth whose memory drives one to despair!

I'm going back to bed; forgive me. I fear I got worked up; yet

I'm not weeping. At times one wanders, doubting the facts, even when one has discovered the secrets of the good life.[43]

No, Clamence is not weeping; he is Europe's shaggy John the Baptist "with dry eyes," who, in the wilderness of a city's gray stones and stagnant canals, makes straight the way for a non-existent messiah. In this moment Clamence lays bare the *déchirement* of what is more than the soul of an individual; the anguish should find its response in every man. But the cardinal fact is that there is nothing tragic here: the tension is not broken as if before an irremediable loss of "islands in the path of the trade winds." Nor is Clamence pathetic: there is no suggestion of his being caught in a situation to which he cannot reply and in which he cannot insert some distant hope. To the very end Clamence plods on in his role of judge-penitent. The tension never lapses.

We said that *The Fall*, in marking a return to self by Camus, actually constituted a reversal of his previous concerns with revolt. We can now make clear just how sharp a reversal this is. It should be remembered that the theme which rings through the works of Camus from the very beginning is the innocence of men; Camus, from *Noces* onward, has defended the innocence of men against those theologies, ideologies, and regimes which would treat mankind as guilty. The whole call to revolt is a call to an innocent state in which all that is of value is within a man and all that is evil is outside him. This constant proclamation of the rebel's inner innocence and goodness and the outside world's oppressive evil has been the lyrical touchstone for much of Camus' writing and is given its fullest development in *L'Homme révolté*. But the question which must eventually be put to Camus and which he must put to himself is this: If, in revolt, man is innocent before the evil with which he is afflicted, then how do you account for the origin of this evil against which man revolts? Are all men innocent? Obviously not, inasmuch as it is men who create the oppressive conditions against which the rebel revolts. How, then, do you explain the guilt and evil of the men whom the rebel opposes? The theme of human innocence running through Camus' works is, finally, a one-sided theme, a conviction which only emphasizes the incomplete nature of Camus' message. Whence human guilt and evil?

The problem which Camus creates for himself out of his philosophy of revolt is inescapable: It is all very well to speak of the evil outside of men in "others," but to every other man I *am* an "other," and thus how is it that I am a man of guilt and evil as well as of innocence and goodness? To the sensitive reader Camus' almost continual emphasis on the guilt of the external "other" is the prime fault haunting the philosophy of revolt, but in justice to Camus we should note that *The Fall* is not the first indication of his awareness of this other side of the problem. It is in *The Plague* that we first see this aspect of revolt in its full complexity. Here we find Rieux and Tarrou struggling against the external evil of the plague; in relation to the plague they are innocent, they are proponents of goodness. But it is Tarrou who is aware of all that is involved in this; it is he who suggests that the plague is not simply something outside of men but is within them as well, an evil against which they must struggle. Tarrou is keenly aware that in relation to the plague which afflicts him he is innocent. But, simultaneously, in relation to the plague within him he is guilty. This is the contradiction in which he is caught, and it is beyond this that he yearns. It is just this yearning which is carried over into *The Fall*, and *The Fall* constitutes a reversal of Camus' concerns precisely because he is no longer dealing with "I, the innocent rebel" but rather with "I, the guilty 'other.'" This is an entirely new exploration for Camus, the rounding out of the neglected other half of his position. And it is because of its newness as an exploration that Camus has turned up with new tools of a religious, psychological, and introspective nature. The decisiveness of this reversal is no-

175

where reflected more strikingly than in the way in which, in obvious reference to himself, he looks at himself as the innocent and virtuous defender of the oppressed and charges that this defender is actually the evil "other" which he is constantly reviling. The true moral stature of Albert Camus comes into focus in this moment when he confesses, "I am an innocent rebel, but I am much more than this: I am also a guilty evildoer." At this point Camus' philosophy of revolt becomes both complex and profound. And at this point Camus submits his thought to a tension which it has never before known and a yearning which was never before so anguished.

In *The Fall* we discover more sharply than in any other of his works the Camusian scene of a single individual given over to a lucid acceptance of "his times"—an acceptance which lives in this conflict, allowing the social anguish of an historical moment to become the personal anguish of an individual moment. Jean-Baptiste Clamence is a mirror of his times, but not simply this alone: he is the existential embodiment of his times. In a very real sense he *is* the times. There are those philosophers who think of God as being involved in the total historical process while yet standing above it, like a conscience, judging and suffering it. Clamence is, in a sense, this kind of being; he is playing the role of such a God by accepting within himself the rich and conflicting currents of a whole age and not simply living this but suffering it, because a conscience, a sense of rightness and proportion, has been brought into this acceptance. In consciousness of his guilt Clamence suffers the wrongs committed in his paradise. Yet beyond these two conflicting realms of paradise and penitence, he envisions those islands on the high seas which mean innocence and redemption. Without these islands he would not suffer, for there would be nothing finally at stake. What we see here is an illustration of Nietzsche's dictum: If the old tablets of the law have been broken, then we must make new ones. No man can live in absolute freedom. Clamence is a man who forsook his virtue and became free, but complete freedom is an unbearable condition: a new "virtue," a new law had to be found. But there was no such law, and Clamence is left in an interim period, attempting, as a judge-penitent, at least to make it clear to all men exactly what it is in which they are caught. And perhaps by clarifying the problem he has taken the first step toward the creation of the "new law." In Clamence we do not see the "rebel" who has discovered his innate value by virtue of a threat which is external to him; rather, we find a man who, not being involved in a social situation of external threat, discovers that no innate value is forthcoming: taken alone, without being in conflict with the world, Clamence's soul reveals only the unbearable emptiness of freedom. And this is why he longs for the innocence he once knew, while rejecting the virtue he once practiced. Clamence, the mirror of his times, hints that the life of rebellion is not all-sufficing, that it must finally create something out of itself which makes possible an ongoing civilization that can guarantee a certain innocence and peace without being ceaselessly revolted against. Clamence and his age seek an old innocence and a new law.

It is in this way that Clamence suffers: he is the suffering of history. Certainly there is no suffering of history except as it is embodied in an individual. But there is more to this: simply in being what he is, Clamence suffers not just history but *our* history; he suffers it for us. Here we come to his unusual significance: he is essentially a Christ-like figure who accepts the common sins and ills of every man while holding them in tension with the common longing of every man. Like Christ, he suffers for us. And perhaps this is the only kind of Christ that Camus could ever conceive: one who suffered for us without hope or final assurance. Perhaps this is the only Christ possible for an age which has suffered the fall: a poor and stumbling Christ who, in an age before the fall, would be nothing more than a preparer of the way, not worthy to tie the thongs on the sandals of a true Christ. Clamence, whose effort it is to lead men to a certain penitence and a certain righteousness, is clearing a path which becomes overgrown almost as soon as he has finished. He recognizes the situation he is in, knows that "It's too late now. It will always be too late. Fortunately!" He knows himself and his age and knows the difficulty of his task, and yet he plods on. He can do no other. He lives in a time when there can be only a preparation and never a completion. But it is the duty of a man to remain true to those things he knows to be true: his own searing conflict and a yearning for the islands. If history forbids hope and if human nature withholds promise, this is no matter. The essential task is to hold fast to one's truth and one's reality. All else will take care of itself.

In Clamence's narrative the profoundly religious concern of Camus comes into the thick confusion of our history like light filtering through the tangle of a jungle. This religious concern is "profound" precisely because it is at grips not with religious doctrines and practices but rather with the fundamental human condition out of which religions arise. Clamence may be a kind of Christ in our time, but to say this is not to imply that Camus has given over to Christian faith. No, Camus is at grips with the abiding human problems out of which the Christian faith sprang and to which it responded. *The Fall* goes far toward reopening a debate to which the Christian faith has given the last and best rejoinder. The question seems to be roughly this: Given the inescapability of personal guilt and judgment, how may one go beyond guilt and judgment to attain the blessedness of innocence? Put even more traditionally, the question is: How can my existence find justification? In this strange monologue of a troubled modern conscience an ancient question has somehow been struck and tossed up. Clamence is a man who has absorbed all the blows that a modern man can absorb, yet he stands beyond either a tragic end or a pathetic ongoing. He stands burdened and tense, troubled by the yearning which has already found voice in other of Camus' pages: How can one become a saint without God? It seems that ultimately this is the only question worth asking. There is no answer given, and Clamence must go on holding out the question and preserving his tension unflinchingly.

Much of Camus' genius and power comes from the way in which he competes with the Christian faith on its own ground. His concerns are not so much Christian as pre-Christian in nature, and he stands alongside Kierkegaard and Nietzsche as a thinker who is convinced that the advent of the "modern world" has brought with it novel problems and novel insights which force us to look again at the abiding condition of men in a way which was not fully possible for the first Christians. Without any doubt this is the reason for the profound and disturbing appeal which Camus, as well as his two forebears, has for our time. In challenging the Jewish-Christian heritage and in taking up again the problems to which it responded, he has touched upon that painfully suppressed conviction that the Jewish-Christian heritage can no longer inspire or support individuals and their culture, and that hence we must turn our thoughts once more to the fundamental reality of a world in which men are born, find suffering and happiness, and die. In *The Fall* Camus has put his finger on the anguish of an age. And we see that Clamence and the tension in which he lives and waits is not something unusual in the world of Camus; rather, it is typical of this world and essential to it, for, after all, Clamence can only be described in the same terms in which we have originally characterized Camus himself when it was said that he was "the most acute conscience of the contradictions of our times between the nihilism of destruction and the nostalgia for peace."

CHAPTER X
A LAST WORD ABOUT
REVOLT

WITHIN any cogent philosophical position there is a conception or conviction which gives that position its recognizable character and without which that position cannot be understood. This would apply to any system of thought whether it be highly rational and systematic, such as that of Thomas Aquinas or Hegel, or whether it be highly subjective and prophetic, such as that of Kierkegaard or Friedrich Nietzsche. The problem of understanding a philosophical position involves first of all, its characterization; after this we may examine the position for its coherency or cogency. In this study of the thought of Albert Camus we have been concerned primarily with this latter task, to wit, that of presenting the thought of Camus in its totality and analyzing his thought into its various concerns, themes, and truth judgments so as to see what is coherent and what is not. We come now to the task of characterizing that thought and indicating what is the primary conception or conviction which motivates it. We should say at once that this is not a simple matter. For this study of the philosophy of Albert Camus has revealed that there are conflicts in his thought that, in analysis, divide his philosophical career into two contrasting bodies of thought. One may take the absurdist experiment or one may take the philosophy of limits, but one cannot take both. Nor can Albert Camus take both. Because of these difficulties, our first question is this: "Is there a conception or conviction which motivates and characterizes the total thought of Albert Camus?" On the basis of the study made of Camus' thought our answer would be that there is not. But before developing this answer it would be wise to review three notable efforts which have been made to characterize the total thought of Camus according to a single theme. These are the efforts of Francis Jeanson, Pierre-Henri Simon, and Rachel Bespaloff who, respectively, characterize the philosophy of Albert Camus by the themes of (1) absurdity, (2) happiness, and (3) death.

Francis Jeanson, in his critique of *L'Homme révolté*, took exception to Camus' denunciation of revolutionary history, as being a withdrawal from all historical action in favor of man's dignity in his "dialogue with the Absurd." He sums up the movement of Camus' thought from *Noces* to *L'Homme révolté* as a movement away from and then back to the purity of this dialogue with absurdity; Camus' brief concern with history is seen by Jeanson as the determined effort to prove once and for all that historical action is futile, i.e.,

Doubtlessly, the Mediterranean heritage hardly predisposed him in this direction [that of historical action]. Seen from the African beaches, history as such is confused with "the history of European pride," which is only an interminable nocturnal delirium. Sisyphus already knew that he should not allow himself to be caught in the trap of action: one must act, to be sure, but simply for the sake of acting and without expecting any result, without nourishing the illusion of giving meaning to that which cannot have it. Even so, the *Résistance* must have opened a breach in the system through which several illusions penetrated: With the Liberation Camus thought he felt at ease with history to the point that he undertook to moralize it. The Revolution was on the march; it was going to be pure and noble. But this idyll does not last: in fact history was only an unfaithful wench, more inclined to violence than to the language of virtues; it was time to begin the rupture. It is in 1947 that Camus began writing *L'Homme révolté*.[1]

Although Francis Jeanson is not a Communist, it should be recognized that his estimate of Albert Camus is largely that of Communist writers as well as many Socialists. This viewpoint contends that the reaction to the absurdity of the universe has simply been extended to include the absurdity of history and all revolutionary action. Camus is seen to begin and end in a sterile, solipsistic confrontation with the Absurd. In reply to this estimate of Camus, it is correct to say that these critics have not understood the transition from *The Myth* to the philosophy of revolt. They have not seen that the absurdity which has been posited of the world, *has not* been also posited of men in history. The world is absurd, because it is unlike man, but history is not absurd because it is made by men. Jeanson has not seen the specific distinction between *The Plague* and *The State of Siege*: man may never defeat the tendency toward injustice and murder that all men carry in their hearts, but this is not to say that men may not, in revolt, destroy an oppressive regime and replace it with a moderate regime which respects the limits of the human condition. From another perspective we may note that Camus, from the individualist position of *The Myth*, does not condemn the world for its irrationality but simply points out the ultimate importance of the absurd confrontation which arises between man and the world; he does not condemn the world, because *the world is what it is*, and its difference from man offers no basis for a judgment of the world as such. But in the case of the oppression which man faces at the hands of murderous regimes and ideologies, Camus condemns these things, because they are the creations of men who have betrayed the "is" of the human condition, its limits and needs. And this condemnation is possible, because in human history there is a basis for judgment, a value which is implicit in human nature. Camus contends that when this value is betrayed it manifests itself in human revolt, a revolt which is of men and against that which threatens all men. Hence, if Camus has accused the revolutions of the 20th century of betraying the earth-bound solidarity which men have discovered in modern times, then he does so on the basis of a value which he believes is historically evident in human nature. Jeanson's critique is irrelevant, inasmuch as it ignores the value theory which is central to *L'Homme révolté*. It is incumbent upon Jeanson and any Marxist critics to meet Camus' proposition that all political societies must respect the values and limits of human nature, lest they oppress man and eventually be judged and destroyed by this value which they will awaken to the fury of revolt. Absurdity does not explain the thought of Albert Camus, for revolt has surpassed this stage.

Pierre-Henri Simon, in his series of lectures entitled *Temoins de l'homme*, has an admirable concluding lecture on Albert Camus. Simon feels that Camus stands alone among modern writers in possessing a positive humanism, a humanism which recognizes the absurdity of the world but attempts to find something beyond this. This "something beyond" is, acording to Simon, the happiness which Camus seeks, i.e.,

> Moreover it should not escape us that, by virtue of the awakening, the progress toward wisdom is distinguished in no way from the search for happiness. The question of happiness is constantly posed in the work of Camus. . . . In his most despairing moments Camus never loses sight of the great task of man which is to learn to be happy, and he clearly thinks that the absurd man, he who has become conscious of the nonsense of everything, is better disposed than anyone else to live intensely and to know happiness.[2]

And later Simon says,

> This austere philosopher who has been called stoical, and who in fact is, by a certain bent of mind, is not a somber and wailing philosopher; he knows that man is made for happiness, and he seeks to show him the possible ways.[3]

Simon's characterization of Camus' thought as a search for happiness is shared as well by Andre Rousseaux.[4] In considering this point of view we should hark back to the figure of Tarrou in *The Plague*. Tarrou wanted to be a saint without God; at the end of this struggle with the forces of the plague he hoped that there might be peace. In short, Tarrou desired happiness in place of or in spite of the torment and revolt which were the substance of his life. But Tarrou died in the midst of the struggle and never found this happiness. At the instant of his death his face still showed the tension of his revolt and his strength. Tarrou may have been capable of finding the happiness that he craved, but his desire was, from the beginning, thwarted by his revolt against the "plague" that is in men and in societies. His life was devoted to a struggle in behalf of the oppressed, and in choosing such a life he chose the contradiction, tension, and agony which would forever make peace impossible. How could the rebel be happy when others suffer? This is what Caligula suddenly realized, i.e., that "men die and they are not happy." Happiness is the sacrifice which a man makes to the imperative value of revolt.

In terms of Camus' philosophy, "happiness" is the existential equivalent of unity and order. And it is true to say that this is an integral part of his thought. But it is quite untrue to say that this is the central theme of his thought. All men have this nostalgia for unity which is rooted in their very natures, but both in the universe and in human history this nostalgia goes unsatisfied. That the world does not satisfy this nostalgia is a truth which Camus accepts, but that human history thwarts this need for unity and solidarity is not to be accepted, it is to be revolted against. In Camus' mature philosophy of limits, man's demand for unity takes its place in a dialectical relation with man's protest and, thus, constitutes the phenomenon of revolt. To say that unity is the dominant term is to deny the need for man's negative protest. Man does, by his nature, desire unity, but he is man-in-the-world, and his need for unity brings him into rebellious conflict with the ignorance, intractability, and folly of human history. If man be in the world, then his desire for unity means a protest against disunity, and his protest against this condition means that he holds the demand for unity. Neither can be separated, for they gain their dialectical unity within the process of revolt. Hence, the characterization of Camus' thought simply as a search for unity is impossible; it is partially that, but not wholly so. The central concern is revolt. It is evident that this understanding which Simon brings to the philosophy of Camus is founded on the view that Sisyphus is still the dominant figure in this philosophy. But Sisyphus was not *in* the movement of human history; he stood alone and beleaguered against the empty heavens. However, in the philosophy of limits, Sisyphus has discovered other men and has taken part in their revolt. From this discovery onward, Sisyphus' happiness was profoundly transformed.

Rachel Bespaloff's "Le Monde du condamné à mort," written shortly before her death, constitutes one of the most penetrating critical essays yet written on Camus' thought.[5] This essay has the basic assumption that the motivating concept of Camus' philosophy is that all men are condemned to death. She puts this as follows, i.e.,

But let us remember that the central theme of his works is condemnation to death. It little matters here whether this be nature, destiny, justice, or human cruelty which pronounces the sentence. We well know that in his most diabolical inventions man only imitates the tortures of life. In principle, the act of inflicting death without accepting the risk of dying establishes the physical and metaphysical basis for torture, to the measure in which it transforms a human being into a thing. . . . The penalty of death which awakened Tarrou to his vocation may seem anodyne next to the horrors of the plague. It was a question of making us feel that there is no essential difference.[6]

In a previous section of this study there was a discussion of the manner in which Camus' reflections on the significance of death have been a guiding concern in both the early and later phases of his philosophy. The earlier absurdist phase had reflected on "my" death, whereas the later thought began with the problem of the inflicted death of others. And it is true to say that the individual's problem of being condemned to die is the dominant theme of the works of Camus up to the play, *Caligula*. But Rachel Bespaloff means to say that this same theme continues through the essay. "Remarque sur la révolte," the journalistic pieces, *The Plague, The State of Siege,* and *The Fall,* which is to say that man faces certain death not only as a creature of the universe, but also as a creature of history. She recognizes the new elements of revolt and the solidarity of men around a common value, but does not see that this does any more than expand the notion of condemnation to death. To establish this contention Mme. Bespaloff has centered her attention on the early works of Camus, especially *The Misunderstanding,* and on one work in the *révolté* period, *The Plague.* It is the very general meaning which the "plague" is given that makes it possible for Mme. Bespaloff to feel that the earlier concern with certain death is reaffirmed in the *révolté* thought of *The Plague.* But she can maintain this thesis only by ignoring every other writing which has come from the pen of Camus since 1945, that is, since the play, *Caligula.* If one understands these writings, he will realize that the oppression and death which many men of the 20th century meet within totalitarian states is met by Camus not with an attitude of resignation but with a philosophy of revolt. The cosmic pessimism which characterizes *The Myth* cannot be found in the hopeful revolt which characterizes the philosophy of limits. The terror and death which totalitarian regimes bring to men is not the inevitable lot of men; it is a betrayal of the common nature of men. And precisely because it is a betrayal, there are grounds for its defeat. In short, Mme. Bespaloff has not understood that "essential dimension" of human experience which is revolt. The earlier obsession with the inevitability of death has not been negated in Camus' later thought; it has been surpassed. The absurdist experiment itself was found to be sterile. That all men shall die is a problem we can do nothing about. That all men shall be oppressed is a problem we can do something about, and this is the beginning of the philosophy of revolt.

All three of these attempts to characterize the total thought of Albert Camus according to a single theme are unsatisfactory, because they become entangled in the contradictions between the absurdist experiment and the philosophy of limits. In each case the themes of the absurdist experiment are taken as definitive and the effort is made to incorporate them into the philosophy of limits. And in each instance it was found that these themes could be understood only in the larger, controlling context of the idea of revolt.

There is the authentic thought of Albert Camus with which this study has begun and ended, and there is the *raisonnement absurde* which stands apart from this. It is in this authentic line of thought that Camus continues his philosophical task, and the fact that a section of his earlier thought is independent only serves to emphasize the searching, exploratory character of his thinking. Camus' authentic philosophy is one of revolt, or perhaps it is better to say his method is one of revolt. Revolt is the theme and feeling which dominates this thought, with its two terms and its tension, with its uncertain universe and its certain death, with its protest against gods and tyrants and its struggle to create unity and values, with its ceaseless change, contradiction, and surpassment, with its intense fidelity to the human condition. To understand revolt is to understand man in the world, for here all the attributes of the world and of man find their focus and meaning in the revolt of *this* man, at this *moment*. We cannot admire or be repulsed by this thought without admiring or disliking their creator. These are the thoughts of a man who is passionately concerned with what he argues, and who cannot be disentangled from these issues. When he speaks of death, he means *his* death; when he speaks of a yearning for peace and solidarity, he means *his* yearning; when he speaks of man's revolt, he means *his* revolt. These problems are not indifferent, they are compelling and ultimate; they are, for Camus, tormenting problems which can be answered only through an intense and honest inquiry into which one throws his whole being. Camus' works are more like confessions than philosophical essays; they are the disturbing revelations of a man who is painfully involved in the contradictions of our times. The intimate relation between the man, Albert Camus, and his works is perhaps suggested in this statement of his, i.e.,

> I am not a philosopher, in fact I can only speak of what I have lived. I have lived nihilism, contradiction, violence, and the dizziness of destruction. But, at the same time, I have greeted the power to create and the honor of living. Nothing gives me the right to judge from above an epoch of which I am completely a part. I judge it from within, confusing myself with it. But I hold to the right of saying, henceforth, what I know about myself and others, only on the condition that this may not add to the unbearable misery of the world, but rather will indicate, in the dark walls against which we grope, the yet invisible places where the gates may open. Yes, I hold to the right of saying what I know, and I shall say it. I am only interested in the renaissance.[7]

The "two or three ideas" which Camus has made his own are simple ideas and do not grow into a complex philosophical system. Despite the simplicity of his ideas, they become extraordinary when coupled with Camus' demand that they be lived to the limits of what human passion can reach. In Camus' thought, the truth value of an idea can never be rationally developed to a point of satisfaction; ideas are substantiated only in human experience and action. In Camus' philosophy, truth is revealed in what has been called a "dialectical-dramatic" form, in the ongoing tension of human ideas and human passion. Hence, the developing thought of Albert Camus is not to be considered as a pilgrimage which drives relentlessly toward its goal; for there is no such goal. The value which man seeks is not in the future, nor is it beyond his ken; it is within man, part of his nature, and is to be found and incarnated only in the creative tension of the passionate life. The philosophical career of Albert Camus has been a running battle with life and with the ideas of his times, and this battle goes on within the limits which make up the human condition, within this proportion which rests in the nature common to all men. It is here that he finds his value, and it is this value which he throws against life.

FOOTNOTES

FOOTNOTES

INTRODUCTION

1. J.-P. Sartre, "Response à Albert Camus," *Les Temps Modernes*, August, 1952, p. 338.
2. A comment by Germaine Brée in "Albert Camus and The Plague," *Yale French Studies*, No. 8, p. 93.
3. P. Néraud de Boisdeffre, "Albert Camus ou l'expérience tragique," *Etudes*, December, 1950, p. 303.
4. P.-H. Simon, "Albert Camus et l'homme," *Temoins de l'Homme* (Paris: Librairie Armand Colin, 1951), pp. 176-77.
5. Jean Wahl, *Esquisse pour une histoire de "l'Existentialisme"* (Paris: L'Arche, 1949).
6. Paul Tillich, "Existential Philosophy," *Journal of the History of Ideas*, January, 1944, pp. 44-70.

CHAPTER I

1. Albert Camus, *Noces* (Paris: Gallimard, 1950), p. 35.
2. *Ibid.*, p. 16.
3. *Ibid.*, p. 80.
4. *Ibid.*, p. 81.
5. *Ibid.*, p. 63.
6. *Ibid.*
7. *Ibid.*, pp. 34-35.
8. *Ibid.*, pp. 81-82.
9. *Ibid.*, pp. 85-86.
10. *Ibid.*, pp. 89-90.
11. *Ibid.*, p. 92.

CHAPTER II

1. Albert Camus, *Le Mythe de Sisyphe* (Paris: Gallimard, 1942), p. 15.
2. *Ibid.*, pp. 21-22.
3. Cf., Paul Tillich, "Existential Philosophy," *op. cit.*, pp. 51-55.
4. Camus, *Le Mythe de Sisyphe*, *op. cit.*, p. 27.
5. *Ibid.*, p. 29.
6. *Ibid.*, p. 30.
7. *Ibid.*, p. 11.
8. Albert Camus, *Actuelles: Chroniques 1944-1948* (Paris: Gallimard, 1950), p. 112.
9. Camus, *Le Mythe*, *op. cit.*, cf. pp. 38-45 for this review of "desert thinking."

10. *Ibid.,* p. 45.

11. Shestov (1866-1938), whose real name was Schwarzman, emigrated from Kiev to Paris after the Bolshevik Revolution.

12. *Ibid.,* p. 60.

13. *Ibid.,* p. 61.

14. *Ibid.,* p. 60.

15. *Ibid.,* p. 54.

16. *Ibid.,* pp. 73-74.

17. Contrast this with James Collins' curious statement that Camus' theory is "that suicide is the only logical attitude in an absurd world . . ." which shows the surprising misconceptions that are often attributed to Camus' thought; *The Existentialists* (Chicago: Henry Regnery Co.), p. 117.

18. Camus, *Le Mythe, op. cit.,* pp. 85 f.

19. *Ibid.,* p. 88.

20. *Ibid.,* p. 88.

21. *Ibid.,* p. 154.

22. *Ibid.,* p. 125.

23. *Ibid.,* p. 131.

24. *Ibid.,* pp. 154-55.

25. *Ibid.,* p. 157.

26. *Ibid.,* p. 168.

CHAPTER III

1. Albert Camus, *The Stranger,* trans. Stuart Gilbert (New York: Alfred A. Knopf, 1946), p. 72.

2. *Ibid.,* p. 123

3. J.-P. Sartre, "Explication de *L'Etranger,*" *Situations,* I (Paris: Gallimard, 1947), pp. 110-111.

4. *Ibid.,* p. 99.

5. *Ibid.,* pp. 120-121.

6. *Ibid.,* pp. 109-110

7. This viewpoint has been confirmed by Camus in private conversation with the author.

8. Camus, *Le Mythe de Sisyphe, op. cit.,* p. 27.

9. Camus, *The Stranger, op. cit.,* pp. 126-27.

10. *Ibid.,* p. 112.

11. *Ibid.,* p. 87.

12. *Ibid.,* pp. 2, 9, 10, 20, 29, 60, 66, 72, 73, 74, 75.

13. *Ibid.,* p. 66.

14. *Ibid.,* p. 72. (Italics my own)

15. *Ibid.,* p. 74.

16. *Ibid.,* pp. 75-76.

17. *Ibid.,* pp. 151-152.

18. *Ibid.*, p. 153.

19. *Ibid.*, p. 154.

20. *Ibid.*

21. Leon Thoorens, *A La rencontre de Albert Camus* (Paris: La Sixaine, 1946), p. 10.

22. Albert Camus, *Le Malentendu, suivi de Caligula* (Paris: Gallimard, 1947).

23. Camus, *The Stranger, op. cit.*, pp. 99-100.

24. Camus, *Le Malentendu, op. cit.*, p. 23.

25. *Ibid.*, p. 16.

26. Thoorens, *op. cit.*, p. 37.

27. Camus, *Le Malentendu, op. cit.*, p. 61.

28. *Ibid.*, p. 49.

29. *Ibid.*, p. 73.

30. *Ibid.*, p. 74.

31. *Ibid.*, p. 79.

32. *Ibid.*, p. 81.

33. *Ibid.*, p. 61.

34. *Ibid.*, pp. 84-85.

35. *Ibid.*, p. 95.

36. Camus, *Noces, op. cit.*, p. 30.

37. *Ibid.*, p. 86.

38. Albert Camus, *Le Malentendu, suivi de Caligula, op. cit.*

39. *Caligula* was first staged in 1945, a year later than *The Misunderstanding*, but, surprisingly enough, it was written in 1938, the year when Camus began preparation of both *The Stranger* and *The Myth*. We choose to treat it at this point because, despite its earlier composition, it forms a natural bridge from the Absurd to the philosophy of revolt. Even in 1938 Camus had dramatically illustrated the limitations of the absurd line of reasoning.

40. *Ibid.*, pp. 108-109.

41. *Ibid.*, p. 110.

42. *Ibid.*, p. 111.

43. *Ibid.*

44. *Ibid.*, p. 179.

45. *Ibid.*

46. Albert Camus, "Remarque sur la révolte," *L'Existence*, ed. Jean Grenier (Paris: Gallimard, 1945).

47. Camus, *Caligula, op. cit.*, pp. 210-211.

48. Robert de Luppé, *Albert Camus* (Paris: Editions Universitaires, 1952), p. 104.

CHAPTER IV

1. Cf. Robert de Luppé, *op. cit.*, pp. 67 ff., and Leon Thoorens,

op. cit., p. 19. This error is found as well in the two studies on Camus by the Frenchmen, Roger Quilliot and Albert Maquet, which the reader will find listed in the bibliography.

2. Michel Mohrt, "Ethic and Poetry in the Work of Camus," *Yale French Studies*, Spring-Summer, 1948, p. 115.

3. *Ibid.*, pp. 115-116.

4. Manuel de Dièguez, *De L'Absurde* (Paris: Editions du Triolet, 1948), pp. 9-21. These remarks of Dièguez are interesting also for their indication of the enormous effect which *The Myth of Sisyphus* had among students of post-war France.

5. A. N. Whitehead, *Process and Reality* (New York: The Social Science Book Store, 1929), p. 89.

6. Camus, "Remarque sur la révolte," *op. cit.*, pp. 11-12.

7. *Ibid.*, p. 23, the underlining is my own.

8. Albert Camus, *Actuelles II* (Paris: Gallimard, 1953), p. 83.

9. *Ibid.*, p. 35. A complete disavowal of this earlier position can be found in Camus' *L'Eté* (Paris: Gallimard, 1954), pp. 132-33.

10. Albert Camus, *The Rebel*, trans. Anthony Bower (New York: Alfred A. Knopf, 1954), p. 16.

11. *Ibid.*, p. 17.

CHAPTER V

1. Albert Camus, "Remarque sur la révolte," *L'Existence*, ed. Jean Grenier (Paris: Gallimard, 1945).

2. *Ibid.*, p. 15.

3. Camus, *Actuelles II*, *op. cit.*, p. 32.

4. Camus, "Remarque sur la révolte," *op. cit.*, p. 19.

5. Albert Camus, *L'Homme révolté* (Paris: Gallimard, 1951), pp. 35-36.

6. *Ibid.*, p. 36.

CHAPTER VI

1. *Ibid.*, p. 67.

2. *Ibid.*

3. *Ibid.*, p. 80.

4. *Ibid.*, p. 81.

5. *Ibid.*, p. 105.

6. *Ibid.*, p. 101.

7. *Ibid.*, p. 114. Cf. also Camus' open letter to André Breton in *Actuelles II*, *op. cit.*, pp. 39 ff.

8. *Ibid.*, p. 126.

9. *Ibid.*, p. 128.
10. *Ibid.*, p. 129.
11. *Ibid.*, p. 130.
12. *Ibid.*, p. 152.
13. *Ibid.*, pp. 154-55.
14. *Ibid.*, p. 184.
15. *Ibid.*, p. 186.
16. *Ibid.*, pp. 190-205.
17. *Ibid.*, p. 208.
18. Albert Camus, *Les Justes* (Paris: Gallimard, 1950).
19. *Ibid.*, p. 40.
20. *Ibid.*, p. 43.
21. *Ibid.*, pp. 69-70.
22. *Ibid.*, p. 73.
23. *Ibid.*, p. 101.
24. *Ibid.*, p. 132.
25. *Ibid.*, p. 147.
26. *Ibid.*, p. 149.
27. *Ibid.*, p. 162.
28. *Ibid.*, p. 168.
29. Camus, *Actuelles II*, *op. cit.*, p. 22.
30. Camus, *L'Homme révolté*, *op. cit.*, pp. 211-12.
31. *Ibid.*, p. 225.
32. Albert Camus, *Lettres à un ami allemand* (Paris: Gallimard, 1948), pp. 78-79.
33. *Ibid.*, p. 85.
34. *Ibid.*, p. 42.
35. Cf. the two editorials written for *Combat*, entitled "Défense de l'intelligence" and "Anniversaire" found in *Actuelles I*, *op. cit.*, pp. 114-19 and pp. 131-35, respectively.
36. Cf. Francis Jeanson, "Albert Camus ou l'âme révolté," *Les Temps Modernes*, May, 1952 (it is the contention of Jeanson that Camus views Marxism solely from its prophetic aspect; he makes the interesting accusation that Camus does not "believe" in substructures).
37. Camus, *L'Homme révolté*, *op. cit.*, p. 236.
38. *Ibid.*, pp. 276-77.
39. *Ibid.*, p. 278.
40. *Ibid.*, p. 295.
41. *Ibid.*, p. 301.

CHAPTER VII

1. Albert Camus, "Le Pain et la liberté," *Actuelles II*, *op. cit.*, pp. 157-72.

2. *Ibid.*, p. 163.

3. A large sampling of these editorials has been published in the volumes, *Actuelles I: Chroniques 1944-1948, op. cit.,* and *Actuelles II; Chroniques 1948-1953, op. cit.* These volumes include as well selected letters, book prefaces, speeches, and interviews.

4. Camus, *Actuelles II, op. cit.,* p. 174.

5. Camus, *L'Homme révolté, op. cit.,* p. 348.

6. *Ibid.*, p. 357.

7. *Ibid.*, p. 361.

8. *Ibid.*, p. 361.

9. Camus, *Actuelles I, op. cit.,* p. 22.

10. *Ibid.*, pp. 48-52.

11. *Ibid.*, pp. 45-47.

12. *Ibid.*, pp. 48-52.

13. *Ibid.*, pp. 59-62.

14. *Ibid.*, pp. 63-66.

15. *Ibid.*, pp. 94-98.

16. *Ibid.*, pp. 123-126.

17. *Ibid.*, pp. 141-46 and pp. 146-150, respectively.

18. *Ibid.*, p. 145.

19. *Ibid.*, pp. 146-47.

20. *Ibid.*, p. 149.

21. Camus, *Noces, op. cit.,* pp. 47-48.

22. Camus, *Actuelles I, op. cit.,* pp. 150-54 and pp. 155-59, respectively.

23. *Ibid.*, p. 159.

24. *Ibid.*, pp. 160-64 and pp. 165-69, respectively.

25. *Ibid.*, p. 159.

26. "A New Social Contract," pp. 169-74 and "Toward Dialogue," pp. 175-79, *ibid.*

27. *Ibid.*, p. 179.

28. Cf., *ibid.*, pp. 183-207.

29. Cf. Camus, *Actuelles II, op. cit.,* pp. 69-76.

30. Jeanson's critique, "Albert Camus ou l'âme révolté" is found in *Les Temps Modernes,* May, 1952, pp. 2070-2090; the response of Camus, Sartre, and Jeanson's rejoinder are all found in the August, 1952 issue of the same journal. This same letter of Camus, bearing the title "Révolte et servitude," has been reprinted in *Actuelles II, op. cit.,* pp. 85-124.

31. For a full discussion of this aspect of Camus' thought see my article, "Albert Camus and the Christian Faith," *The Journal of Religion,* October, 1956, pp. 224-33.

32. As examples of critical remarks concerning Camus' attitude toward the Christian faith, see P. N. de Boisdeffre, "Albert Camus ou l'expérience tragique," *Etudes,* December, 1950, pp. 316 ff.;

and P.-H. Simon, "Albert Camus et l'homme," *Temoins de l'Homme* (Paris: Librairie Armand Colin, 1951), pp. 192-93.

33. Camus, *L'Homme révolté, op. cit.*, p. 363.
34. *Ibid.*, p. 364.
35. *Ibid.*, p. 364.
36. *Ibid.*, p. 365.
37. *Ibid.*, p. 367.
38. Camus, *Actuelles II, op. cit.*, pp. 166-67.
39. *Ibid.*, p. 36.
40. Camus, *Lettres à un ami allemand, op. cit.*, p. 42.
41. Camus, *L'Homme révolté, op. cit.*, p. 337.

CHAPTER VIII

1. Camus, *L'Homme révolté, op. cit.*, p. 313.
2. *Ibid.*, p. 316.
3. *Ibid.*, p. 319.
4. *Ibid.*, p. 335. In Camus' *The Fall*, discussed in the following chapter, we find an extraordinary example of this "most anguished cry" caught in the "tautest language."
5. Camus, *Le Mythe de Sisyphe, op. cit.*, p. 131.
6. Camus, *Noces, op. cit.*, p. 34.
7. This was the task of *The Plague*.
8. Camus, *L'Homme révolté, op. cit.*, p. 334. For other writings relevant to Camus' esthetic theory, cf. "Le Temoin de la liberté," *Actuelles I, op. cit.*, pp. 253-67; "Le Pain et la liberté," *Actuelles II, op. cit.*, pp. 157-72; "L'Artiste et son temps," *ibid.*, pp. 173-82.

CHAPTER IX

1. P. N. de Boisdeffre, "Albert Camus ou l'expérience tragique," *Etudes*, December, 1950, p. 314.
2. Germaine Brée, "Albert Camus and *The Plague*," *Yale French Studies*, No. 8, p. 95.
3. Michel Mohrt, "Ethic and Poetry in the Work of Camus," *Yale French Studies*, Spring-Summer, 1948, p. 117.
4. Rachel Bespaloff, "Le Monde du condamné à mort," *Esprit*, January, 1950, p. 9.
5. Camus, *Actuelles II, op. cit.*, p. 94.
6. Camus, *Actuelles I, op. cit.*, p. 249.
7. Albert Camus, *The Plague*, trans. Stuart Gilbert (New York: Alfred A. Knopf, 1952).
8. Simon, "Albert Camus et l'homme," *op. cit.*, p. 192.
9. Camus, *The Plague, op. cit.*, p. 6.

10. *Ibid.*, pp. 11-12.
11. *Ibid.*, pp. 87-88.
12. *Ibid.*, p. 196.
13. *Ibid.*, pp. 196-97.
14. Cf. the address, "L'Incroyant et les chrétiens," given by Camus in a Dominican convent on the theme of the dialogue needed between Christians and non-Christians, *Actuelles I, op. cit.*, pp. 211-219.
15. Camus, *The Plague, op. cit.*, p. 200.
16. *Ibid.*, p. 201.
17. *Ibid.*, p. 227.
18. *Ibid.*, pp. 228-29.
19. *Ibid.*, p. 229.
20. Bespaloff, *op. cit.*, p. 16.
21. Camus, *The Plague, op. cit.*, pp. 230-31.
22. *Ibid.*, pp. 262-63.
23. *Ibid.*, pp. 277-78.
24. *Ibid.*, p. 278.
25. *Ibid.*
26. P.-H. Simon, *op. cit.*, p. 109.
27. Albert Camus, *L'Etat de siège* (Paris: Gallimard, 1948).
28. Camus, *Actuelles I, op. cit.*, p. 242.
29. Cf. Camus' preface to *l'Espagne libre*, edit. Georges Bataille (Paris: Calmann-Levy Editeurs, 1946); also Camus, *Actuelles II, op. cit.*, pp. 135-45.
30. Camus, *L'Etat de siège, op. cit.*, pp. 50-51.
31. *Ibid.*, pp. 89-90.
32. *Ibid.*, pp. 175-76.
33. *Ibid.*, p. 212.
34. *Ibid.*, p. 214.
35. *Ibid.*, p. 232.
36. Camus, *The Rebel, op. cit.*, p. 273.
37. Albert Camus, *The Fall*, trans. Justin O'Brien (New York: Alfred A. Knopf, 1957).
38. *Ibid.*, pp. 139-40.
39. *Ibid.*, p. 136.
40. Albert Camus, "La Mer au plus près," *L'Eté* (Paris: Gallimard, 1954).
41. *Ibid.*, p. 170.
42. *Ibid.*, p. 181.
43. Camus, *The Fall*, op. cit., p. 144.

CHAPTER X

1. Jeanson, *op. cit.*, p. 2084.

2. Simon, *op. cit.*, p. 183.

3. *Ibid.*, p. 184.

4. Andre Rousseaux, "Albert Camus et la philosophie du bonheur," *Littérature du XXe siècle* (Paris: Albin Michel, 1949).

5. The insight and provocativeness of her brief article is admirable; it far excels, so it seems to us, that of any of the four book-length studies on Camus which have appeared in France.

6. Bespaloff, *op. cit.*, pp. 9-10.

7. *Actuelles II*, *op. cit.*, p. 83.

BIBLIOGRAPHY

BIBLIOGRAPHY

WORKS BY ALBERT CAMUS

(in chronological order)

Camus, Albert. *Noces.* Paris: Gallimard, 1950 (published originally in 1938).
——. *L'Etranger.* Paris: Gallimard, 1942.
——. *The Stranger.* Translated by Stuart Gilbert. New York: Alfred A. Knopf, 1953.
——. *Le Mythe de Sisyphe.* Paris: Gallimard, 1942.
——. *Le Malentendu, suivi de Caligula.* Paris: Gallimard, 1947.
——. *Lettres à un ami allemand.* Paris: Gallimard, 1945.
——. "Remarque sur la révolte," *L'Existence.* Edited by Jean Grenier. Paris: Gallimard, 1945.
——. "Preface," *L'Espagne libre.* Edited by Georges Battaile. Paris: Calmann-Levy Editeurs, 1946.
——. *La Peste.* Paris: Gallimard, 1947.
——. *The Plague.* Translated by Stuart Gilbert. New York: Alfred A. Knopf. 1952.
——. *L'Etat de siège.* Paris: Gallimard, 1948.
——. *Actuelles: Chroniques 1944-1948.* Paris: Gallimard, 1950.
——. *Les Justes.* Paris: Gallimard, 1950.
——. *L'Homme révolté.* Paris: Gallimard, 1951.
——. *The Rebel.* Translated by Anthony Bower. New York: Alfred A. Knopf, 1954.
——. *Actuelles II: Chroniques 1948-1953.* Paris: Gallimard, 1953.
——. *L'Eté.* Paris: Gallimard, 1954.
——. *La Chute.* Paris: Gallimard, 1956.
——. *The Fall.* Translated by Justin O'Brien. New York: Alfred A. Knopf, 1957.

BOOKS AND ARTICLES ABOUT ALBERT CAMUS

Albérès, R. M. "Albert Camus et le mythe de Promethée," *La Révolte des ecrivains d'aujourd'hui.* Paris: Editions Correa, 1949, pp. 65-81.
Astorg, Bertrand d'. "De La Peste et d'un nouvel humanisme," *Aspects de la littérature européenne depuis 1945.* Paris: Editions du Seuil, 1952, pp. 191-200.
Bespaloff, Rachel. "Le Monde du condamné à mort," *Esprit,* January, 1950, pp. 1-26.
Brée, Germaine. "Albert Camus and *The Plague,*" *Yale French Studies,* No. 8, pp. 93-100.

Dièguez, Manuel de. *De l'Absurde*. Paris: Editions du Triolet, 1948, pp. 9-21.

Hanna, Thomas. "Albert Camus and the Christian Faith," *The Journal of Religion*, October, 1956, pp. 224-33.

Jeanson, Francis. "Albert Camus ou l'âme révolté," *Les Temps Modernes*, May, 1952, pp. 2070-2090.

Luppé, Robert de. *Albert Camus*. Paris: Editions Universitaires, 1952.

Maquet, Albert. *Albert Camus ou l'invincible été*. Paris: Nouvelles Editions Debresse, 1955.

Mohrt, Michel. "Ethic and Poetry in the Work of Camus," *Yale French Studies*, Spring-Summer, 1948, pp. 113-118.

Mounier, Emmanuel. "Albert Camus ou l'appel des humiliés," *Esprit*, January, 1950, pp. 27-66.

Néraud de Boisdeffre, Pierre. "Albert Camus ou l'expérience tragique," *Etudes*, December, 1950, pp. 303-325.

Quilliot, Roger. *La Mer et les prisons: Essai sur Albert Camus*. Paris: Gallimard, 1956.

Rousseaux, André. "Albert Camus et la philosophie du bonheur," *Littérature du XXᵉ siècle*. Paris: Albin Michel, 1949.

Sartre, Jean-Paul. "Explication de *l'Etranger*," *Situations, I*. Paris: Gallimard, 1947, pp. 99-121.

——. "Reponse à Albert Camus," *Les Temps Modernes*, August, 1952, pp. 334-53.

Simon, Pierre-Henri. "Albert Camus et l'homme," *Temoins de l'homme*. Paris: Librairie Armand Colin, 1951, pp. 175-93.

Thoorens, Leon. *A la rencontre de Albert Camus*. Paris: La Sixaine, 1946.

Collins, James. *The Existentialists: A Critical Study*. Chicago: Henry Regnery Co., 1952.

Tillich, Paul. "Existential Philosophy," *Journal of the History of Ideas*, January, 1944, pp. 44-70.

Wahl, Jean. *Esquisse pour une Histoire de "l'Existentialisme."* Paris: L'Arche, 1949.